T0355259

EIGHTEEN TAKES ON GOD

Eighteen Takes on God

A SHORT GUIDE FOR THOSE WHO ARE STILL PERPLEXED

Leslie Stevenson

OXFORD
UNIVERSITY PRESS

OXFORD
UNIVERSITY PRESS

Oxford University Press is a department of the University of Oxford. It furthers
the University's objective of excellence in research, scholarship, and education
by publishing worldwide. Oxford is a registered trade mark of Oxford University
Press in the UK and certain other countries.

Published in the United States of America by Oxford University Press
198 Madison Avenue, New York, NY 10016, United States of America.

Library of Congress Cataloging-in-Publication Data
Names: Stevenson, Leslie, author.
Title: Eighteen takes on God : a short guide for those who are still perplexed /
Leslie Stevenson.
Description: [New York, New York] : [Oxford University Press], [2019]
Identifiers: LCCN 2019015293| ISBN 9780190066109 (hardback) |
ISBN 9780190066130 (etext) | ISBN 9780190066116 (updf) |
ISBN 9780190066123 (epub)
Subjects: LCSH: Theism. | God.
Classification: LCC BL200 .S74 2019 | DDC 211—dc23
LC record available at https://lccn.loc.gov/2019015293

1 3 5 7 9 8 6 4 2

Printed by Integrated Books International, United States of America

CONTENTS

PART III: EXPERIENCES

PREFACE

I am not writing for theologians or philosophers, though I can hardly stop them reading this little book if they feel so inclined. (I am no theologian, though I have dipped a toe in some of the stuff in recent years.) This book is meant for anyone who feels perplexed about the very idea of God. Anyone who feels quite *certain* about the topic (whether for or against) might learn something if they are prepared to open their minds a bit. I aim to offer a brief and clear guide to some of the main conceptions of God down the centuries, along with my own comments.

On this topic we had all better acknowledge there can be no such thing as a completely detached, neutral, objective approach. Everyone has their own upbringing, their life experiences, prejudices, and commitments to (or rejections of) religious traditions they have encountered. And whole cultures diverge: there are anciently entrenched differences between Jewish, Christian, and Islamic monotheisms; there are some theistic strands in Hinduism and Buddhism. Moreover, there are rival views *within* all these traditions.

I confess to having been an academic philosopher (now retired), but my aim here is to present the ideas and arguments in a style that presupposes nothing except interest and intelligence. I offer the reader two levels of engagement: the main text can be read without digressing into the endnotes, which contain digressions, more esoteric or academic material, and suggestions for further study. Perhaps more has been written about God than anything else over the centuries, and I am conscious of how little of it anyone can hope to take in: I merely hope to assist readers' thought about my selection of topics.

The three parts proceed in approximately decreasing order of intellectuality. Part I reviews eight realist conceptions of God in fairly philosophical fashion. Part II examines some accounts of religious language that tend toward non-realist interpretations of God. Part III tries to get nearer to real-life religion, and my own commitments will begin to show. But there is no need to let the cat out of the bag here, readers can judge its felinity and felicity for themselves. Religious attitudes and convictions can change over a lifetime; in writing this I have clarified my own views, but I do not regard them as final. These eighteen "takes" are not full-blown doctrines or theories, but images or snapshots from different points of view. Whether they are all of the *same* God, I leave the reader to puzzle over.

My biblical quotations are from *The Oxford Study Bible* (New York: Oxford University Press, 1992).

EIGHTEEN TAKES ON GOD

PART I

CONCEPTS

This first part will be somewhat intellectual, as I set to review and critique a varied set of influential conceptions or theories of God. I cannot claim to cover more than a judicious selection of what has been written on this subject. I am not writing for academic theologians or philosophers of religion, or for students of those subjects, though I would be pleased if they find anything useful. To the gentler, non-specialist, perhaps less committed readers I promise I will try to say something about real-life religion, but it will not emerge on center stage until Part III.

THE OLD MAN IN THE SKY?

From the opening creation story in the Hebrew Bible to the closing apocalyptic vision of a new heaven and a new earth in the Christian New Testament, there is language about God which, if taken at face value, implies that he inhabits a human body (usually male) and performs physical actions like ours. (I acknowledge feminist sensibilities, but I can see no convenient way of avoiding male pronouns for God throughout this book). At *Genesis* 3:8 Adam and Eve heard the sound of the Lord God *walking about* in the garden at the time of the evening breeze; at *Exodus* 33:23 God allows Moses to *see his back* but not his face; in *Psalm* 18:8 we read "Smoke went up from his *nostrils*, devouring fire from his *mouth*"; at *Isaiah* 6:1 the prophet "*saw the Lord seated* on a throne, high and exalted, and the skirt of his robe filled the temple"; at *Zephaniah* 3:17 "the Lord your God will *shout* with joy" (in some translations he *sings*); and at *Revelation* 21:5 the "One" who *sat on the throne* and *said* "I am making all things new" is surely God.[1] Images of gods and goddesses in human (or animal or hybrid) form are found in many ancient cultures all around the world such as Egypt, India, and the Aztecs.[2] An ancient Greek historian remarked how the different human races represent their gods in ways resembling themselves. In Homer's *Iliad* the Greek gods intervene in human affairs, sometimes intimately.[3]

Although Jewish monotheism has texts that suggest some kind of embodiment for God, the second commandment forbids the making of visual images of the deity: "You must not make a carved image for yourself, nor the likeness of anything in the heavens above, or on the earth below, or in the waters under the earth" *(Exodus* 20:4). Islam has always maintained a very strict ban on image making, and even the Eastern Orthodox Christianity of Byzantium, famous for its icons, went through a century of iconoclasm. Christian dogma maintains that God was incarnate in Jesus, and Christian imagery has represented Jesus as teaching, healing, crucified, dead, and resurrected. Pictures of God the Father have been less common, though he figures in an occasional stained-glass window. The Holy Spirit is not usually depicted as human but was described as descending in the form of a dove on the occasion of Jesus's baptism *(Mark* 1:10), and "tongues of fire" conveying the Holy Spirit were said to touch each of the apostles *(Acts* 2:3). The doctrine of the Trinity, that God is three persons or personalities forming in some sense a society, is represented in the famous Russian icon by Andre Rublev *The Hospitality of Abraham: The Holy Trinity* in which three mysterious robed and winged androgynous human figures with reverently inclined heads seem to send a loving glance around the circle. The point was surely not literal picturing, but visual symbolization of the doctrine of the triune nature of God.[4]

Despite the biblical ban on graven images, some prominent strands of Christian art have risked visual representations of God himself, at least since the Renaissance.[5] On the ceiling of the Sistine Chapel in the Vatican, Michelangelo (1475–1564) was commissioned (and presumably well rewarded) to paint God as a bearded figure of a certain age leaning out of a rather crowded dark cloud outstretching his index finger, at the tip of which floats the newly created Adam. Perhaps the idea was to represent how effortless creation was for God. Such images have affected many people's conception of God ever since, as in those familiar cartoons of a white-bearded gent sitting frowning on a cloud.

The effect has been reinforced by the striking images created by William Blake (1757–1827), such as *The Ancient of Days* in which we see another formidably bearded elderly patriarch caught in the act of creation, this time wielding a compass as an apparent nod to scientific modernity (though Blake's intention was apparently to express his romantic visionary *rejection* of the Newtonian mathematical account of the physical world). In *Elohim Creating Adam* he equipped his God with an enormous pair of wings (looking far too heavy for flight), apparently rescuing Adam from a snake writhing around his legs.[6] These images by Michelangelo and Blake have been widely reprinted by publishers on the covers of books about religion, even when their authors reject any such grossly anthropomorphic ideas.

Visual imagery remains influential in literate cultures like ours, and it was more so in nonliterate times as ancient icon-painters, medieval sculptors, stained-glass designers, and Renaissance popes well knew (as do modern-day television and film producers, advertising directors, and political campaigners). With screens in our living rooms and at our fingertips we are bombarded with imagery these days, and corporations and products identify themselves by their logos. Adverts and social media can fix an image in our minds which may forever afterward represent a concept to us. If you ask your neighborhood atheist what *conception* of God she is rejecting, a common answer may be that mythical old fellow giving out commandments, observing human affairs disapprovingly, throwing down thunderbolts, and perhaps performing the occasional miracle—an image that owes as least as much to ancient Greek stories of Zeus than to the God of the Bible.

But whatever crude beliefs there may have been in the anthropological past and may persist in some quarters, classic and contemporary theologians (Jewish, Christian, or Muslim) certainly do *not* understand God to be a physically embodied person (however dignified, powerful, masculine, or bearded) who occupies a particular portion of space, exerting power like a human potentate, king, or pope but to an exalted or infinite degree.[7] Would such a God last for only a finite time and be mortal like us? And how could he be the creator of the whole material universe, if he himself is one part of it?

The influential twentieth-century philosopher Ludwig Wittgenstein (1889–1953) is recorded as saying of Michelangelo's painting: "If we ever saw this, we certainly wouldn't think this the Deity. The picture has to be used in an entirely different way if we are to call the man in that queer blanket 'God.' "[8] What that different way could be remains to be seen (perhaps in the rest of this book), but Wittgenstein's main point was surely that the picture should not be interpreted as a visual likeness of God. Oliver Cromwell sternly commanded his artist to paint him "warts and all," but if God does not literally have a face there is no question of making a portrait of him (with or without warts).

There are biblical passages that represent God as speaking from a mountain or from heaven (*Exodus* 19:3–9, *Mark* 1:11, *Luke* 9:34–5), as sitting on a throne, as riding through the sky breathing fire, or more gently, as a shepherd (*Psalm* 23)—though not all at once. But we surely do not need to understand these words literally. The Psalms and much of the prophetic writings are poetic (the clue is in their linguistic form), and it is characteristic of poetry to use *verbal* imagery, especially metaphorical uses of words. Nobody believes that the Lord is literally their shepherd, or that they themselves are sheep to be led in green pastures and fed on grass: the idea is obviously that the Lord cares for us in something *like* the way a good shepherd looks after his flock. Respect for the scriptures does not involve taking everything in them literally: but that leaves us with questions how to interpret those apparently non-poetic, literal, historical passages in which God is represented as speaking and acting in the world of human affairs—questions I will touch on in subsequent chapters.

For my money, more genuinely spiritual art is found in the Dutch interiors of Johannes Vermeer (1632–1675), in the early landscapes of Samuel Palmer (1805–1881), and in some of the paintings of Vincent van Gogh (1853–1890). None of them depict God or anything explicitly theological, but they can be seen as expressing the glory of God. Vermeer's religious convictions may be unknown, but he presents us with carefully composed, meticulously painted, ordinary domestic scenes of a girl reading or a servant pouring milk, yet invested with a strange and intense beauty (of the whole scene, rather than the human figure); these are paintings that invite and reward extended contemplation. Palmer was a deeply religious man who regarded his artistic work as part of his spiritual life. In a series of remarkable images, such as *The Bright Cloud* (reproduced on the front cover of this book) and *Cornfield by Moonlight with the Evening Star*, he transfigured the preindustrial rural landscapes around the village of Shoreham in Kent with an extraordinary radiant intensity, in which humans and their animals and agriculture appear as part of the natural world.[9] Van Gogh's vigorously executed oil paintings depict a cornfield, cypress trees, the stars, a bedroom chair, or even a pair of old boots with a different style of intensity. All three artists imbue ordinary scenes with an extraordinary beauty and mystery that leads us beyond the visual, without any attempt to explicitly represent anything beyond.

I take it, then, that we are not to interpret the *physical* imagery and language about God literally. But how should we understand the even more prevalent human-like *mental* descriptions of him? I take up this question in the next chapter.

2

THE OMNIPRESENT PERSON

Serious conceptions of the creator God of Judaism, Christianity, and Islam are not physically anthropomorphic. Nevertheless, much scripture and theological tradition has thought of God as a *person* (a unique, more than human person, of course) who does not have a body, does not occupy one part of space or live for a finite time, yet is in some sense present everywhere and at all times. God has also been described as a "spirit," meaning a center of consciousness and intelligence and will, who knows (by a non-bodily kind of perception) what happens in the world, who reacts to it with moral judgment (and perhaps emotion?), and is able (by some non-bodily kind of action) to cause changes in the world.

The Bible and the Qur'an are full of ascriptions of mental states, decisions, and actions to God: here is a representative selection.[1] In *Genesis* 3:8–19 God *realizes* that Adam and Eve have eaten the fruit he has forbidden, and because of that he *sentences* them to a life of hard agricultural labor and childbearing labor. At *Genesis* 6:5–8 God is *horrified* by the wickedness of humankind, he bitterly *regrets* his creation, and *resolves* to wipe them off the face of the earth, except Noah and his family. In *Isaiah* 1:11–28 God says he is *fed up* with the Israelites' sacrificial offerings of animals, he *loathes* their festivals, and he *threatens* to wreak vengeance on his enemies, though prepared to *forgive* those who are willing to obey him. Similar themes reverberate throughout the rest of the prophetic books. The epistles of Paul proclaim God's just *judgment* on sin (*Romans* 1:18–2:16) and crucially his *designation* of Jesus Christ to be the means of human liberation from sin (*Romans* 3:21–31, 5:1–21). In the Qur'an God is represented as *knowing* all things— "what enters the earth and what comes out of it; what descends from the sky and what ascends to it." He *sees* all that people do and whatever is in every heart (57:2–6), he *provides* all the good things that sustain life (16:1–16), but he is *displeased* with our ingratitude (80:17–32), he may *punish* evildoers (16:45–7), yet is prepared to accept repentance and *forgive* sins (40:3).

Theologians and philosophers in the three Abrahamic religions have tried to formulate in intellectual terms the conception of God they find explicit or implicit in their sacred scriptures. I will be looking at some of their ideas in subsequent chapters, starting here with the idea that though God does not inhabit a physical body he is, quite literally, the subject of a variety of *mental* states, including knowledge; moral judgment; anger or righteous indignation; attitudes of love, forgiveness, and mercy; and intention and will in bringing about effects in the world.[2]

Let us look first at William Blake's poem *The Divine Image*:

To Mercy, Pity, Peace, and Love
All pray in their distress;
And to these virtues of delight
Return their thankfulness.

For Mercy, Pity, Peace, and Love
Is God, our father dear,
And Mercy, Pity, Peace, and Love
Is Man, his child and care.

For Mercy has a human heart,
Pity a human face,
And Love, the human form divine,
And Peace, the human dress.

Then every man, of every clime,
That prays in his distress,
Prays to the human form divine,
Love, Mercy, Pity, Peace.

And all must love the human form,
In heathen, Turk, or Jew;
Where Mercy, Love, and Pity dwell
There God is dwelling too.

Blake represents the divine in human terms, valorizing mercy, pity, peace, and love. He was affirming the goodness of human life (and of animal life, in other poems) over against the dehumanizing effect of industrialism and child exploitation of which he was vividly aware (nor have these evils disappeared even now). But philosophers and theologians may tend to worry in their literal-minded way about just what conception of God is implicit in the poem. Blake does not say explicitly that God is merciful, loving, pitying, and peaceful, rather that the combination of these admirable qualities (capitalized like Platonic Forms) "is God," and that wherever they are present in *any* person, regardless of theological belief, God is present too. A skeptical reader (such as Feuerbach, see Chapter 10) could say that this amounts only to saying that mercy, love, pity, and peace are beautiful ideals that we project onto a supposed superhuman person, and that the real point is that we must do our utmost to realize these ideals in human life. On that view there is no need for belief that God is literally a person.

Theologians may say that human beings are made in the image of God (very imperfectly, everyone has to admit), rather than God being made in the image of humans (even if idealized). They may admit that our *ideas* of God are formed in one way or another from our human experience, as all our ideas about anything surely are; but they will insist that what our best ideas of God refer to, namely *God himself*, is the ultimate reality—and is in some important sense personal. The twentieth-century Oxford philosopher of religion Richard Swinburne introduced his fairly standard conception of God as follows:

> *a person without a body (i.e. a spirit) who is eternal, free, able to do anything, knows everything, is perfectly good, is the proper object of human worship and obedience, the creator and sustainer of the universe.*[3]

Alvin Plantinga, an influential Christian philosopher in the United
States, assumed at the outset of his different philosophical defense
of Christian belief much the same *conception* of God as a superhuman person:

> God is a person; that is, a being with intellect and
> will . . . God is thus all-knowing and all-powerful; he is
> also perfectly good and wholly loving. Still further, he has
> created the universe and constantly upholds and provi-
> dentially guides it.[4]

For both these thinkers (and many more) God is invisible and in-
tangible, yet he is a person or "spirit," possessing supreme knowledge, will, power, and goodness—admirable human capacities and
qualities raised to an infinite degree.[5] (That requires more than a
finite body and brain, however large and impressive, bearded, or
winged!)

There are philosophical questions about how an incorporeal
spirit or person can *perceive* the world and *act* within it. These are
causal notions: human perception involves the impact of the environment on our sense organs, and our actions and speech are
the effects of our intentions and decisions, via our limbs and
lips. How then are we to conceive of divine perception and action without a body? Of course, many cultures and people down
the ages have believed in incorporeal spirits or gods who perceive and affect things—but that anthropological fact does not

prove the idea to be coherent. It has been a common *illusion* to apply concepts of mentality in inappropriate cases, e.g. to "see" intentions or meaning in the stars or comets, in eclipses, plagues, climatic changes, and thunderbolts. Even now we have a tendency to misapply our evolved mental module for recognizing other people and interpreting their mental states—for example seeing a face in the fire, hearing a voice in the wind, or losing our temper with a malfunctioning car as in one of John Cleese's memorable scenes. Modern monotheists will reject such superstitions and illusions but want to retain God as a very special case for mental attributions. If challenged about the nature of God's mentality, a common reply is that his ways are not our ways, so how he perceives the world and acts in it must be accepted "in faith" as a mystery beyond our understanding.

Perhaps this is more a matter of fundamental *feeling* about the meaning of the world and of human life than intellectual assent to a metaphysical proposition. G. K. Chesterton summed up his own attitude as follows:[6]

> *Thus ends, in unavoidable inadequacy, the attempt to utter the unutterable things. These are my ultimate attitudes towards life; the soils for the seeds of doctrine. . . . I felt in my bones, first, that this world does not explain itself. . . . The thing is magic, true or false. Second, I came to feel as if magic must have a meaning, and meaning must have some one to mean it. There was something personal in the*

> world. . . . Third, I thought this purpose beautiful in its
> old design. . . . Fourth, that the proper form of thanks to
> it is some form of humility and restraint.[7]

But as with Blake's poem, there seems to be room for the attitudes
without the personalist metaphysics. Can't an atheist marvel in
the sheer existence of the world in all its variety, especially those
aspects that many of us may see as beautiful or "magical" or in
some sense "meaningful"? The inference to "someone who means
it" will not seem compulsory to everyone.

Skeptical critics may say that the move from the embodied
conception 1 to the incorporeal personal conception 2 is the re-
placement of something ludicrously false by something meaning-
less. But the philosophical project of setting limits to meaningfulness
has itself proved a difficult and controversial matter. Much poetic
language will not pass the test of empirical verifiability or falsifia-
bility (i.e., as assertions about the material world that can be tested
by observation), but poetry can surely be meaningful in other
ways. Most believers are reluctant to concede that their apparently
factual claims about the fundamentally divine nature of the universe are "merely" poetic; and, in any case, we should question the
assumption that poetry cannot convey anything serious. We find
ourselves confronted here with deep and difficult questions about
language, meaning, and alleged limits to human conception or
knowledge. I will be taking up some of them in Part II.

God's incorporeal *knowledge* has often been seen as less of
a problem than his action, for we seem able to conceive of an

all-seeing, immediate, and omniscient awareness of everything that happens. *Psalm* 139 contains an extended meditation on God's omniscience not just of our deeds but our very thoughts, emotions, and desires: "Lord, you have examined me and you know me. You know me at rest and in action; you discern my thoughts from afar." In these days of CCTV, satellite photography, and Internet hacking, we can more readily imagine a worldwide intelligence-gathering web feeding real-time data about everything that happens into a single supercomputer, with a single divine mind watching the screen (well, not literally *watching*, but receiving the information in some non-bodily way). Such surveillance by the state or corporations or manipulators of political campaigns sounds sinister, and even the idea of a loving parent knowing about *everything* one gets up to is not unambiguously attractive. The idea of omniscience is only tolerable when combined with discretion, emotional stability, unconditional love, and readiness to forgive (which sets the bar very high for parents). A reductionist interpretation of the idea of divine knowledge of our minds would be that there are *facts* about our thoughts, emotions, attitudes, and intentions, and they *matter*—for they constitute what we are and have consequences in our behavior.

The idea of divine *action* involves further complexities and problems. Action surely implies causing things to happen that would not otherwise have happened, so it may seem that God's actions would make exceptions to the normal course of events governed by the laws of nature. Many believers continue to use the scriptural language about God creating, speaking, acting, redeeming, and judging, which seems to imply that he exists *in time*, going through mental changes. I will take up these themes of divine temporality and action in Chapter 8.

Theists like Swinburne and Plantinga assume that we can think of God's mentality as disembodied yet sufficiently comparable to ours to be describable using human terms, in the form of similes, analogies, and metaphors. The Lord is not literally my shepherd (that can be agreed on all sides), but if he looks after me rather *like* a shepherd, that seems to imply that he *knows* about my desires and my perils, and that he somehow *acts* to meet my needs and save me from dangers as they arise. The Psalmist declared that God's omniscient knowledge "is beyond my grasp . . . so lofty that I cannot reach it" (139:6). But the theologians cannot explain *how* God manages to be omniscient about our mental states, they just seem to find that thought intuitively convincing.

As we have seen, God has been traditionally conceived of as a person (of a unique cosmic nature), yet other theologians have declared with equal confidence that he is *not* a person. According to Sallie McFague:

> *God is not a "person" or "personal" as such; this model does not cease to be a metaphor merely because it is a more inclusive model than many others in the tradition.*[8]

And Nicholas Lash has written even more definitively:

> *We address God as "you," and speak of God as "him" rather than "it," not because God is "a person" (which he certainly is not, for he is not an anything).*[9]

As our discussion proceeds we will find other religious thinkers who not only maintain that God is not a person but that he is also not any sort of *thing*, substance, or entity: not one more item (however unique) to be listed along with everything else in a catalogue of all that exists.

If serious theologians can disagree so flatly about whether God is a person, aggressive critics may conclude that they do not know what they are talking about. There is also a division *within* those who agree that God is a person, between "evidentialists" like Swinburne who assume that belief in such a divine person needs empirical evidence, and those like Plantinga who claim that Christian belief can be held as "properly basic" without need of any such evidence.[10] Thus there are disagreements not only about whether God exists, and whether he is a person, but also about how we are supposed to *know* anything of him. There is more than enough subject matter for the rest of this little book.

3

THE UNCHANGEABLE
NECESSARY BEING

A highly metaphysical conception of God was developed with considerable sophistication in the Middle Ages. It involved a synthesis of Greek philosophy with Semitic monotheism, and in this case the most influential Greek thinker was Aristotle (384–322 BCE).[1] Much credit for this development is due to the philosopher-theologians of the Islamic Golden Age (roughly, the ninth to the thirteenth centuries) when Islamic civilization, science, and intellectual culture in the Middle East, North Africa, and Spain was in advance of Europe. Muslim scholars had rediscovered the works of Aristotle that had been lost to the West; they studied them deeply and constructed elaborate intellectual systems on the twin basis of Platonic/Aristotelean metaphysics and the teaching of the Qur'an revealed to the Prophet Muhammad in seventh-century Arabia. By the twelfth and thirteenth centuries, these ideas influenced leading Jewish and Christian thinkers such as Maimonides and Aquinas.

Aristotle's conception of the divine was cosmological rather than moral, impersonal rather than personal, and eternal rather than active. In his view the universe as a whole cannot be either created or destroyed, despite the manifold changes within it. He developed the highly influential theory that to explain all the movements in the cosmos, there must be a single underlying and unchanging cause, the Unmoved (or Prime) Mover.[2] In Aristotle's impersonal Prime Mover there is no distinction between actuality and potentiality, or existence and essence: he (or rather *it*?) exists by necessity and cannot change. But although this conception was said to be in some sense divine, this god (if that is the right term) has no knowledge or consciousness of the world, is not concerned with it, and cannot be said to love it or to intervene in it like the Hebrew Yahweh or the Christian "Father."

One of the most original and influential of the Muslim thinkers was Ibn Sina (Latin name Avicenna, ca. 980–1037),[3] a multitalented polymath who contributed to medicine and many other sciences besides philosophy and theology. He studied the works of Aristotle more deeply than anyone in his time (and many since), and he argued for a synthesis of Aristotelean philosophy with Islamic theology. (After his time, much Islamic thought—like some strands of Christian and Jewish theology—has reacted against such attempts to integrate divine "revelation" with human reason.) Ibn Sina argued on Aristotelean lines that since every change in the world has a cause, and there cannot be an infinite regress or a circle in the chain of causes, there must be a supreme cause of everything that is not itself caused but exists necessarily and unchanging. The obvious difference is that Ibn Sina identified this Unmoved Mover as the God (Allah) who spoke to Muhammad.

The great Jewish theologian Maimonides (1135–1204), born in Cordoba in Spain when it was still under Muslim rule, offered further variation on these themes.[4] He endorsed the argument of an Unmoved Mover but maintained (against Aristotle and Ibn Sina) that whether the universe has a beginning in time is not provable by reason alone but is to be believed on the authority of scripture.[5] He held that absolutely everything is subject to the free will of God. But if God is conceived as necessary and unchanging, it surely follows that he cannot acquire new knowledge of human affairs as history unfolds, and does not become angry and punish, or feel compassion and decide to forgive. Maimonides accordingly proposed a radically nonliteral interpretation of the scriptural talk of God's knowledge, providential care, and action.[6] On his view there is nothing in common between our knowledge and God's, we may use the same word but there is a huge difference in what we are talking about, so our only literal descriptions of God are negative.[7] In some rabbinic circles this was deemed unscriptural and heretical.

It was Thomas Aquinas (1225–1274) who developed the most systematic, comprehensive, and precise exposition of this classic medieval conception of God.[8] Since the language we use about God is derived from our knowledge of the created things we observe in the world, including ourselves, none of it literally applies to him. Nevertheless Aquinas maintained that we can apply our human words such as "knowledge," "love," "action," and "will" to God in an *analogous* sense, and thereby attain a limited kind of knowledge of him.[9] Some of our knowledge of God comes from our use of reason, but much of it from his self-revelation in sacred scripture, yet those texts have literal and spiritual meanings which need distinguishing.[10]

According to Aquinas, God is perfect, infinite, unified, and immutable; he is a necessary being in the sense that he does not change; he cannot come into existence or cease to exist. He is transcendent yet immanent, i.e., present and operating in all things. This led to the rather surprising doctrine that God is *simple*. That does not mean that he has learning difficulties or that he is easy to understand; nor does it appear consistent with the doctrine of the Trinity according to which God has three persons or personalities. The most obvious meaning is that God is not composite in any way: since he does not have a physical body, he is without spatial parts or organs (which are subject to injury and disease, and tend to wear out); and since he is changeless, he is not composed of temporal stages like climate change or long-lasting human institutions.[11] Theologians in this classical tradition continue to maintain that God is simple, but this venerable *doctrine* is itself far from simple, it is a complex and sophisticated intellectual construction that is surely puzzling to most believers. It still finds its defenders,[12] but one theologian recently wrote:

> I think the idea of divine simplicity is not a revealed
> or Biblically-grounded supposition. It follows from a

certain sort of philosophical demand that God must be
a complete explanation for everything . . . not a de-
mand which weighs very heavily with most Christian
believers . . . it seems vastly implausible to assert that
something totally simple could explain how such vast
complexity exists.[13]

In the previous chapter we found disagreement about whether
God is a person, now we find dispute about whether he is simple.
Once again it appears that there is more than one conception of
God on the theological market.

Aquinas famously offered five "ways" of proving the existence of God, which are variations on the theme developed by his
intellectual predecessors, namely the requirement for an Unmoved
Mover to be the cause, explanation, or ground of everything that
happens in the world.[14] Many versions of this "cosmological argument" talk of a *first* cause, suggesting thereby a beginning of the
universe in time, followed by subsequent stages of the cosmos and
human history as in the opening chapters of *Genesis*, if read literally. If God's creation is limited to starting off the whole show, we
have a deist conception, to be discussed in Chapter 7. However,
there is a deeper interpretation of divine creation *not* as a one-off
initiatory act but an ongoing relationship by which God sustains
the whole world in existence. On this conception his creative activity explains why the world continues to exist and to operate
as it does. An imperfect analogy might be the input of air, water,
and food that maintains a human life, as opposed to the birth that

brings a new individual into the world in the first place. We might alternatively imagine an electric or nuclear God who generates the energy that keeps everything going but can presumably make a power cut at any time. Such pictures are fun to play with, but they fail to represent the belief that God is not a particular entity or process within or adjoined to the material world, but a changeless, immaterial, transcendent, and necessarily existing reality.

The Eastern Orthodox philosopher David Bentley Hart has endorsed this classical conception of God with irenic enthusiasm:

> To speak of "God" properly, then—to use the word in a sense consonant with the teachings of orthodox Judaism, Christianity, Islam, Sikhism, Hinduism, Baha'i, a great deal of antique paganism, and so forth—is to speak of the one infinite source of all that is: eternal, omniscient, omnipotent, omnipresent, uncreated, uncaused, perfectly transcendent of all things and for that very reason absolutely immanent to all things. [15]

> God is the source and ground of all being and the wellspring of all consciousness, but also the final cause of all creation, the end toward with all beings are moved. [16]

But what do these impressive words mean? The relation of God to all creation is not supposed to be like that of a craftsman to his artifacts, or of the sun's gravitational field to planetary movement, or even of the initial big bang (according to present-day cosmology) to all the subsequent history of the universe. It is not to be understood as causation by any one item or event within the world, but the continued sustaining of the whole show by a fundamental reality totally distinct from it in kind.[17] That, I take it, was the point of the traditional doctrine of God's creation ex nihilo (from nothing), which puts it beyond the reach of theoretical science. However, it is easier to understand what is *not* intended by this doctrine of continuous creation, or upholding, than what is positively meant. The various words used to indicate God's relation to the world—"source," "ground," "wellspring," "creation," "upholding," "sustaining"—are ordinarily used with water or earthly matter or human actions, so they cannot literally be applied to an immaterial God. Once more we find ourselves straining the limits of language, using words metaphorically or in the hope of achieving some sort of analogical truth.[18]

Hart is remarkably confident about his version of the cosmological argument for the existence of God:

> All physical reality is logically contingent, and the existence of the contingent requires the Absolute as its source. Why the Absolute produces the contingent may be inconceivable for us; but that the contingent can exist only derivatively, receiving its existence from the Absolute is a simple deduction of reason.[19]

> To me, the argument for the reality of God from the contingency of all composite and mutable things seems unarguably true, with an almost analytic obviousness.[20]

But not everyone finds this inference so obvious and rationally compelling. The implication is that if God did not continue to sustain the world, it would cease to exist. But how are we are supposed to know the truth of that remarkable counterfactual statement? We cannot have experience or scientific knowledge of worlds going in or out of existence when deprived of divine sustenance, so it seems that we are just expected to "intuit" an alleged necessity. That was the point of Kant's (somewhat turgid) criticism of the cosmological argument for the existence of God which claims that if anything exists, an absolutely necessary being must exist.[21] He questioned the legitimacy of any such explanatory jump from observable, changeable, contingent things to a postulated unobservable, unchanging cause, and he diagnosed it as based on a deceptive principle:

> The transcendental principle of inferring from the contingent to a cause, which has significance only in the world of sense, but which outside it does not even have a sense. For . . . the principle of causality has no significance at all and no mark of it is use except in the world of sense; here, however, it is supposed to serve precisely to get beyond the world of sense.[22]

In Kant's view, any identification of causes (whether one-off or continuous) has to stay within the limits of experience, i.e., what we can observe by our senses and justify by the methods of empirical science. Perhaps in mere speculation we can form a sort of abstract analogical conception of "an ultimate sustainer of things," but the *existence* of such a putative being cannot be proved by empirical science or by pure reason.[23] Kant reinterpreted the need we may feel for an ultimate explanation as "a regulative principle of reason," i.e., a policy for scientific research to keep on seeking increasingly unified conceptions of nature and its laws, but without prospect of reaching an endpoint of all explanation in an Unmoved Mover or a scientific theory of everything.[24]

Here we come up against another clash of supposedly rational "intuitions," and thus, it seems, further confirmation of the limits of human rationality. Hart, like Aquinas, appeals to a (disputable) use of reason to prove some basic theological claims, but like almost every theologian he acknowledges its limitations:

> I happen to think that reason alone is sufficient to compel assent to some sort of formal theism, at least insofar as reason is to be trusted; but that still leads only to the logical postulate of God, which may carry with it a certain arid certitude, but which is in no sense an actual knowledge of God.[25]

Hart therefore appeals to a very different, experiential, mode, saying that for proof of the reality of God one seeks "a particular experience," "an ever deeper communion with a reality that at once exceeds and underlies all other experiences":

> *To say that God is being, consciousness, and bliss is also to say that he is the one reality in which all our existence, knowledge and love subsist, from which they come and to which they go, and that therefore he is somehow present in even our simplest experience of the world, and is approachable by way of a contemplative and moral refinement of that experience. That is to say, these three words are not only a metaphysical explanation of God, but also a phenomenological explanation of the human encounter with God.*[26]

> *God, according to all the great spiritual traditions, cannot be comprehended by the finite mind but can nevertheless be known in an intimate encounter with his presence—one that requires considerable discipline of the mind and will to achieve, but one also implicit in all ordinary experience (if only one is attentive enough to notice).*[27]

So even this latest defender of the cosmological argument for a necessarily existent God as the ultimate explanation of everything acknowledges that pure reason has a limited role in religious faith, and that for most people experience plays the major role. But his "phenomenological explanation" of experience, while attractive

Concepts

and resonant to some, will be found puzzling and alien by others. Human experience differs, and is variously interpreted. The venerable metaphysical conception of an Unmoved Mover is liable to leave some of us—well, unmoved. Some readers may already have been wanting to say as much. I will discuss some variations on the enormous theme of religious experience and faith in Part III.

4

NEGATIVE
(APOPHATIC) THEOLOGY

As noted in Chapter 2, some recent theologians have rejected talk of God as a person, since such usage wrongly suggests that he is one person amongst others (albeit of a very special kind). Even to think of God as a particular *entity* is said to get things wrong if he is understood as one more *item* to be included in any complete list of existing things when he is rather the unique source or ground of everything in the universe (Chapter 3). If so, the time-worn dispute between theists and atheists should not be understood as a disagreement about whether the universe contains one extra (and extraordinary) person or spirit or being. On this view, we should not understand the word "God" as a proper name of a certain very peculiar individual. In the terminology of the German existentialist philosopher Martin Heidegger (1889–1976), God should be described not as *a being*, but as *"Being"* with a capital B (or "Being-in-itself"). Ponderously deep as that may sound, it is far from clear what it means.[1] It is difficult indeed to carry on our exploration of different conceptions of God without continuing to use the G-word *as if* it is grammatically a proper name, but we had better bear in mind that grammatical appearances can be misleading (see Chapter 13).

We have already encountered difficulties in saying what God positively is. There is an ancient and persisting strand of negative, "apophatic," theology to be found within all three monotheist religions (perhaps in other religions too). The basic idea is that we cannot know what God *is*, so we cannot definitely say he is a person, that he is simple, or that he knows or acts; we can only say what he is *not*. Some of the early church fathers held that God is so unlike everything else that his essence is completely unknowable, and we can know him only indirectly, through his "energies" (whatever *they* are). This approach lives on in Eastern orthodox theology, influenced by the Neo-Platonist Christian writer from the early sixth century who has traditionally rejoiced in the title "Pseudo-Dionysius the Areopagite"[2] who wrote in his *Mystical Theology*:

> *God is not soul or mind, nor does it* [note the neutral pronoun!] *possess imagination, conviction, speech, or understanding . . . it cannot be spoken of and it cannot be grasped by understanding. It is not number or order, greatness or smallness, quality or inequality, similarity or dissimilarity. It is not moveable, moving or at rest. It does not live, nor is it life. It is not substance, nor is it*

> *eternity or time . . . there is no speaking of it, nor name*
> *nor knowledge of it. Darkness and light, error and truth,*
> *it is none of these. It is beyond assertion and denial.*

There could scarcely be a more extreme statement of apophaticism.

Following in that tradition was John Scottus Eriugena, a distinguished ninth-century Irish theologian-philosopher. He described God as "the immovable self-identical one," but negatively as "not literally substance or essence," "beyond being": he is "a nothingness whose real essence is unknown (even to angels), the infinity of infinities beyond all comprehension." (Note how the masculine pronoun persists through the incomprehension!) "So we do not know what God is. God himself does not know what he is, because he is not anything, i.e. not any created thing. Literally God is not, because he transcends being."[3]

Meister Eckhardt was a German mystically inclined theologian and preacher in the thirteenth to fourteenth centuries. He treated the scriptures philosophically as descriptive of fundamental reality and recommended the practice of systematic, progressive reason as the exemplary form of life. Among his more controversial apophatic sayings are "God is pure intellect, not being," and "You should love God as he is: a non-God, a non-spirit, a non-person, a non-image." Eckhardt added more positively, but obscurely: "he is a sheer pure limpid One."[4]

Some sacred architecture and decoration, especially the geometric patterns on the walls of mosques (literal representation being strictly forbidden in Islam) suggests a similarly apophatic quest for spiritual meaning. Some modern abstract art also avoids definite representation but seems to strain toward a wordless transcendent message or meaning. In the paintings of the American artist of Russian Jewish descent Mark Rothko (1903–1970) a glimmer or blurry haze of light emerges from a dark brooding frame or background. He designed a nondenominational chapel in Houston, Texas, walled with a selection of his monumental paintings that rigorously exclude any conventional religious imagery yet invite silent contemplation and meditation. Something similar applies to certain minimalist musical works, like those of the Estonian composer Arvo Part (born 1935) and John Taverner (1944–2013) that stay simple and slow but are very evocative. The silence of Quaker Meetings for Worship (see Chapter 18) can work in a somewhat similar way.

As David Bentley Hart notes, "all the major theistic traditions insist at some point that our language about God consists mostly in conceptual restrictions and fruitful negations."[5] But what is the difference between believing in a God of whom we can know nothing and not believing in God at all? There is a dilemma here for negative theology. Is it the outcome of mystical experience about which nothing whatever can be said? Is the relevant experience like wordless music (with no program notes) or a pregnant silence between people (which does not give birth to speech) or unutterable joy (where one cannot explain what one is joyful about)? (The French have a phrase for it, when they say of a person, a dish, or a wine, that he or she or it has a certain *je ne sais quoi*.) Are we then to give up using any language whatsoever about the divine, not even the putative proper name "God"? (Some Quakers tend in that direction.) At that extreme it looks as if negative theology would cease to be *theology*.

For some that may be a blessed relief, but for others it may miss something important. Religious experiences surely have some sort of conscious content, even if not fully expressible in words. They often seem to be *of something* or indeed *someone*, and the unnamed reality is usually felt to be outside oneself. Religious experiences, like all human experience, are inevitably interpreted in terms of the linguistic and conceptual traditions in which their subjects have been enculturated (see Chapters 12 and 14). People brought up in a Christian tradition have claimed visions of Jesus or Mary, others may report revelations of figures from Jewish or Islamic or Buddhist traditions. Empirical surveys of religious experience have been attempted (notably by William James),[6] but any such studies have to select *some* sort of terminology for conceptualizing their subject matter, and that selection is itself always a debatable matter. Much as broad-minded people might to have it, there is little prospect of appealing to human religious experience as the foundation for theology or as a neutral common denominator between different religions.

It is not surprising, then, that most theologians who have embraced some version of the *via negativa* have rowed back from complete agnosticism and have not given up *all* talk of God. Like Maimonides and Aquinas, they say that on the one hand we have positive but "loose" anthropomorphic descriptions of God, which are not to be taken literally but must be understood metaphorically or analogically—for example, talk of the Lord as a shepherd, or a rock, or a consuming fire. On the other hand, the only *literally* true descriptions of God are said to be negative: that he is *not* a being or existing entity, he does not change, he is not composite, that he does not experience emotions. Such a two-level account of God-language was offered by the sophisticated medieval thinkers in all three monotheist religions, as we have seen in Chapter 3.

Yet many believers and theologians have still wanted to affirm that God in some important sense *acts* in the world. Distinctions have been offered between God's "essence" (how he is "in himself") and his "energies" or "emanations." But more needs to be explained if these are to be more than mere verbal formulas. Judaism, Christianity, and Islam have held as their defining dogmas that God has actively revealed himself though certain crucial historical figures such as Abraham, Moses, Jesus, or Muhammad, and less dramatically through other prophets, martyrs, and saints. It is difficult to see how such claims about divine revelations can be construed except as literal and positive (see Chapter 8).

TRUTH, GOODNESS, AND BEAUTY

There has long been a conception of God as the source or ground of the most fundamental *values* that we recognize—namely truth, goodness, and beauty (the three so-called transcendentals of medieval philosophy). Sometimes God has been practically identified with those values. This sort of conception has twin roots in some of the Hebrew scriptures and in the philosophy of Plato in ancient Greece. In *Proverbs* Chapters 8–9 wisdom is personified, in female form: "The Lord created me the first of his works" (8:22), and "I was at his side each day, his darling and delight" (8:30). In the *Wisdom of Solomon*, wisdom is portrayed as "the flawless mirror of the active power of God, and the image of his goodness" (7:26).[1]

Plato (427–347 BCE) held that there are eternal, unchanging, immaterial "Ideas" or "Forms" that set the standards of truth, goodness, and beauty for everything in this material world, including us.[2] Our minds need to be opened to the supreme reality and perfection of these Forms: in Plato's famous and haunting picture of the human condition we are like prisoners chained up in a dark cave, seeing only shadows, unable to see what is really out there, until we are led out into the light by education and philosophy.[3] In that process of enlightenment we come to realize that none of the material objects we perceive by our senses is exactly straight or circular, so that mathematics (Plato had Euclidean geometry especially in mind) is not about the material world but about immaterial Forms that we can conceive through our minds. In a somewhat similar way, no human individual or society is perfectly good, though we must aspire toward the ideal exemplified by the Form of the Good. Thus mathematics and ethics in their different ways transcend our material biological existence. And our attraction (*eros*) to beautiful bodies and beautiful artworks needs to be transformed into love of the eternal Form of Beauty itself.[4] Plato represented the Good as preeminent among the world of the Forms: it plays an almost God-like role in the *Republic* as the ground of all reality, truth, and goodness. He compared its role to that of the sun as the source of all light in the world; but unlike the Hebrew tradition, he did *not* represent it as a person with knowledge, desires, and will.[5]

St. Augustine (354–430) Christianized the Platonic conception of the Good by combining it with the biblical story of God as a personal being who has revealed himself though the history of Israel and in the person of Christ, who can be addressed in prayer and who responds by illuminating our hearts and minds with divine light and wisdom.[6] In his philosophical dialogue on human freedom Augustine was deeply impressed, like Plato, by our mental ability to recognize unchanging, unassailable truths in mathematics. He ascribed a similar status to wisdom, our (fallible) ability to recognize "the highest good" (or the meaning of life), saying that "wisdom is nothing other than the truth in which the highest good is discerned and acquired." He concluded "there is something more sublime than our mind and reason. Here it is: the truth itself." Then came Augustine's remarkable clincher: "the truth is God himself."[7] But what sense can we make of that?

David Bentley Hart has endorsed a very Augustinian connection, or even identification, of truth, goodness, and beauty with God.[8] This seems to be a rather different conception from that of the Unmoved Mover discussed in Chapter 3; it is more Platonic than Aristotelean. When discussing truth Hart asks, "How could being be pure intelligibility if it were not also pure intelligence— the mind of God, so to speak?" He declares that "the very search for truth is implicitly a search for God (properly defined, that is)" and that God is "the logical order of all reality, the ground both of the subjective rationality of mind and the objective rationality of being."[9] Then comes a surprising twist:

> one cannot meaningfully reject belief in the God of classical theism. If one refuses to believe in God out of one's love of the truth, one affirms the reality of God in that very act of rejection.[10]

By this argument, anyone who believes that truth is a fundamental value that we are obliged to honor is implicitly committed to the reality of God, however much they may protest their agnosticism or atheism. But is this anything more than a verbal trick? The Victorian mathematician and philosopher W. K. Clifford earnestly declared that "It is wrong, always, everywhere and for anyone, to believe anything upon insufficient evidence," and (in a line less often quoted) "Belief, that sacred faculty . . . is not ours for ourselves but for humanity."[11] Hart would surely pick up on that word "sacred" and argue that anyone who deploys it—or the concepts of intrinsic rightness or wrongness, evidential justification or lack of it—is recognizing an objective value for all humanity, and is thereby recognizing (perhaps against themselves, as it were) the existence of God. But Clifford and many others would dig in their heels at that and insist that we can seriously accept objective standards for belief (and norms for action generally) without signing up to any sort of theology.

Hart goes on to say that "it is far harder to deceive oneself than it is possible to believe in ethical imperatives without reference to some sort of absolute 'Goodness as such,'" and "a naturalist morality is a manifest absurdity, something rather on the order of a square circle." He affirms in robust Platonic and Augustinian style that "the good is an eternal reality, a transcendental truth that is ultimately identical with the very essence of God . . . the good is nothing less than God himself."[12] While admitting that someone can be an ethical person without *consciously* believing in God, Hart claims:

> *if there were no God, neither would there be such a thing*
> *as moral truth, nor such a thing as good and evil, nor*
> *such a thing as a moral imperative of any kind.*
>
> *. . . to act out of that need [to see and serve the good*
> *by serving others] is, willingly or unwillingly, to act in*
> *relation to God.*[13]

He treats beauty in similar Platonic and theistic fashion:

> *In the experience of the beautiful, and of its pure for-*
> *tuity, we are granted our most acute, most lucid, and most*
> *splendid encounter with the difference of transcendent*
> *being from the realm of finite beings. . . . All delight in*
> *beauty is adoration of God.*[14]

This again invites the riposte that surely it is possible to believe in objective standards of truth, goodness, and beauty without thereby believing in God. Don't we all accept that there are truths to be discovered and recognized in geology, geography, archeology, and history, in the sciences, and in mathematics?[15] Don't most of us (including many though not all moral philosophers) believe there is some objectivity in ethics, that *some* things are clearly right or clearly wrong (even if others are disputed)? Don't many of us believe that some works of art, music, and literature are great and beautiful (perhaps in some sense *true*) in their own distinctive ways (even if many other artworks are rather less so)?

The cloud of witnesses for truth and goodness and beauty includes many self-declared atheists and agnostics: this is a sociological generalization about contemporary Western societies.

In light of this, the neo-Augustinian thesis may be qualified to say that commitment to objective standards or ideals of truth, goodness, and beauty involves an *implicit* belief in God. The claim could be that there is a *necessary connection* here, even if many people these days do not realize it and resist recognizing it. But at this point we seem to reach another inconclusive stand-off between rival "intuitions." Philosophical theists like Hart claim to discern a necessary connection where reflective atheists or agnostics fail to see one, even when confronted with the best statements of the Augustinian case. Of course, if God is *defined* as truth, goodness, and beauty, the connection is achieved by stipulation, and anyone who recognizes the reality of those three "transcendentals" of medieval philosophy can be effortlessly enrolled into the fold of theism. But that is surely a merely verbal maneuver. Theists may say that God is the *ground* or *source* of truth, goodness, and beauty (i.e., there is a one-way connection from him to them) but may not be so ready to accept that God is literally *identical* with that trio (i.e., the conceptual connection goes both ways). Such an abstract philosophical thesis would be puzzling to many believers.

"Every act *for the sake of* the good is a subversion of the logic of materialism," writes Hart. But to slay the dragon of materialism is not yet to win everybody for theism. By "materialism," or "naturalism," Hart presumably means the belief that everything in the world, including everything about human nature, our desires and feelings, our actions and beliefs, can be explained by the methods of science, ultimately in terms of the motions of matter and energy as governed by the laws of physics (a thesis sometimes labeled "scientism"). But the beauty of Mozart's music cannot be explained by physics, though nothing in the soundwaves of a performance *contradicts* any law of physics: in that sense it is not miraculous, though in another sense we readily say it is. Something similar applies to the architecture of the Taj Mahal, Shakespeare's sonnets, the loving relationship of a mother and child, a courageous defense against injustice (and many lesser examples of those genres). The fact that there are levels of humanly recognizable reality that can neither be expressed or explained in terms of the laws of physics (or chemistry or biology) does not amount to supernaturalism as usually understood. The gestation and birth of a baby may in one sense be called "miraculous," "wonderful," or "marvelous," but in another sense it is one of the most "natural" things in human life. The rejection of scientism or "naturalism" does automatically take us to theism.

Keith Ward is another theologian who (in some of his writing) has tended to identify God with goodness:

> It is not accidental that I have ended by speaking of the Good rather than of God. The idea of God, with its long history of debate and dispute, has been too much overlaid with ideas of a supernatural person. . . . If we could think instead of transcendent goodness . . . we might come nearer to the heart of the classical idea of God.

> *"God"is a symbol for the powers of good, for the possibilities*
> *of goodness in our lives, which can challenge and inspire*
> *and empower us. Some still take talk of God literally, and*
> *think of God as a person who watches over us and hears us*
> *pray. But the reality beneath such symbols and metaphors*
> *is the reality of eternal goodness, which puts our lives, so*
> *often devoted to temporal desires, in question.*[16]

But in this inquiry we have already encountered differences about what the idea of God amounts to. Many theologians will surely want to insist that God is not literally *identical* with transcendent values, but is something or Someone who is the ground or source of such values (whatever that means). Some may say that attractive as Ward's writing is, he here veers dangerously close to the reductionist line taken by Feuerbach which we will consider in Chapter 10.

In the philosophical work of Iris Murdoch (and arguably in some of her novels, too), we find an eloquent and fascinating case of someone who saw a close relation between "God" and "Good," but could never quite bring herself to assert their identity. She wrote "God is (or was) a single perfect transcendent non-representable and necessarily real object of attention."[17] There is nothing about personality, omniscience, creation, or omnipotence there: that description better fits Plato's Form of the Good, which Murdoch prefers to traditional theism. But she argued that moral philosophy needs a central concept that has the characteristics she listed. For her that concept can be called "the Good," since morality needs "a non-dogmatic essentially unformulated faith in the reality of the Good, occasionally connected with experience."[18] But she did not believe in God in the sense of a personal supernatural being who knows, loves, and acts. There is a metaphysical difference between Murdoch and theists like Hart and Ward, but is there any ethical difference?[19]

The twin Judaic and Greek roots of the Augustinian identification of God with objective values have rather come apart in this discussion. The biblical stories of a personal God who reveals himself through particular individuals and events in human history do not sit easily with the Platonic conception of a trio of ideal Forms of truth, goodness, and beauty. A transcendent ideal of ethical perfection can inspire us, as Murdoch eloquently argues, but that is not quite the same as traditional theism.

6

PANTHEISM

A radical reaction to the puzzles about divine essence, action, and self-revelation is to cut the Gordian knot and simply identify God with the whole universe distributed through all space and time. That is to give up on the doctrines of transcendence, creation, and intervention as traditionally understood. Is such "pantheism" just atheism in pious clothing? When the early modern rationalist philosopher Baruch de Spinoza (1632–1677) wrote of "God or Nature" as the same thing, was the G-word mere window dressing?[1]

Spinoza was brought up in the community of Portuguese Sephardic Jews who had found a home in the more tolerant Netherlands after their expulsion from the Iberian Peninsula in the late fifteenth century. Superbly gifted in intellect, the young Spinoza began to read and think for himself and was impressed by the new rational, scientific philosophy of René Descartes (1596–1650), though he was to depart from it in crucial respects. Because of his early views on religion, especially his radical historical approach to scriptural interpretation,[2] he was judged heretical and formally expelled from his Amsterdam synagogue at the age of twenty-four.

Spinoza expounded his complete philosophical system in formidably deductive, quasi-mathematical form in his magnum opus, the *Ethics*,[3] much of which is about metaphysics and mind rather than moral philosophy as usually understood. After his revolutionary treatment of God in Part I (which I will get to in a moment), he propounded a philosophy of mind according to which mind and body are two aspects of the same underlying reality. This was quite different from Descartes's influential dualist theory of mind and body as distinct substances, which allowed for the freedom and immortality of the soul and was thus more acceptable to prevailing theology. Spinoza went on to discuss the nature and strength of human emotions, and in Part V he outlined his understanding of human "blessedness" (that is the ethical bit).

About God, Spinoza *appears* to take over much of the classic theological conception of a necessary, unchangeable being whose essence coincides with existence (discussed in Chapter 3), but he proposed to identify this with the whole of nature, or at least with its fundamental or "infinite" aspects (what we now call "the laws of nature"). On this view, nature (aka "God") cannot begin or cease, and the laws of nature explain everything that happens:

> *I think I have sufficiently shown that from God's supreme*
> *power or infinite nature, infinite things in infinite modes,*
> *that is, all things necessarily flow, or always follow from*

> *the same necessity; in the same manner it also follows*
> *from the nature of a triangle from eternity to eternity*
> *that that the three angles will be equal to two right*
> *angles.*[4]

In this unorthodox sense God can be said to "create" everything that happens, but only by rational necessity as in mathematics: this is not the biblical God who creates everything freely ex nihilo.

In this rationalist vision (which still haunts much science and scientific method) everything that happens has a reason. But those "reasons" do not involve anybody acting *for* a reason, with a purpose in view, they are only impersonal causes—what Aristotle called "efficient" causes:

> *Men commonly suppose that all natural things act like*
> *themselves with an end in view, and . . . they assert with*
> *assurance that God directs all things to a certain end (for*
> *they say that God made all things for man, and man that*
> *he might worship God).*[5]

In Spinoza's view, nature as a whole has no aim, its supposed "final causes" (intentions or purposes) are illusions; the only purposes in the world are *human* purposes.

> *I . . . show that nature has no fixed aim in view, and that*
> *all final causes are merely fabrications of men.*

> *. . . all things in nature proceed eternally from a certain*
> *necessity and with the utmost perfection.*[6]

So there can be no miracles, nature cannot abrogate its own laws and perfection; human belief in divine interventions in the course of nature is due to ignorance and superstition. Despite Spinoza's apparently pious talk of God this has widely been seen as a bleakly atheist view of the absence of divine purpose and providence, and he has been labeled a "hideous atheist" even by those who may have harbored some sympathy for his position.[7] But ever since its formulation in the seventeenth century, when modern science was gathering speed, such a view has been found intellectually compulsory by many.

There is some philosophical ambiguity, however, in what sense Spinoza was a pantheist, or an atheist.[8] Was he identifying God with nature, or was he divinizing nature? How far does he depart from the classic concept of God as the ground or source of everything? If we stick with the metaphysical or cosmological aspect of that conception, leaving out the biblical notions of God's will and actions, then there may not be much difference. For the whole of nature—in modern terms, the big bang, the four fundamental physical forces, the laws of quantum mechanics, the biochemistry of DNA, and the operation of natural selection—can be said to be the "ground" or "source" of everything, including ourselves. A contemporary version of pantheism can say that the universe "created itself" in the big bang, and that it "sustains itself" in existence as matter and energy flow according to the laws of physics. To claim (by the cosmological argument examined in Chapter 3) that there must be a necessary unchangeable, but unknowable, creator *distinct* from the whole material show might be a distinction without a difference, at least until we bring in the idea of divine love and forgiveness (see Chapter 17). The religious importance of the doctrine of divine creation surely lies in its existential and value implications about the meaning of human life rather than in any encroachment on the territories of cosmology and evolutionary biology.

Despite the disguised atheism and the undisguised determinism, such a scientifically minded pantheism can allow a certain rather intellectual sort of spirituality and sense of meaning in human life. Spinoza believed that everything that happens in our minds and bodies is determined, and that our minds and bodies are so intimately connected that they are attributes or aspects of one and the same substance, which we would now call the embodied person. Yet we have a distinctive mental power of *reason*, which is a completely different order from the motion of matter and flow of energy: it is a mental rather than a physical "attribute." According to Spinoza, it is possible for us to acquire increasingly adequate ideas of things: we (some of us at least) can come to represent things as they really are, when science discovers the real essences of material things. We can in principle make predictions of every event, and thus understand exactly why and how everything happens. In Spinoza's hyper-rationalist vision, our greatest blessedness depends on adjusting to this intellectual knowledge of "God" or nature, including our own human nature.

This appeal to our rational powers can find some room for morality and self-control. If we are governed by reason, then we will "desire nothing for ourselves that we do not also desire for the rest of humankind," Spinoza earnestly hoped. Yet notoriously people are not always ruled by reason; we are strongly affected by selfish emotions and desires, as well as by collective identities (as Spinoza found to his cost). Anticipating Freud's psychoanalysis, he argued that we can gain control over our wayward emotions if we can become consciously aware of them and understand their causes.[9] Hence perhaps there can be a humanist ethic and a program of self-knowledge or psychotherapy, maybe even some degree of remedy for what has traditionally been called "sin."

Theorizing about human progress took a quasi-pantheist form in the grandiose philosophical system worked out in the extensive writings of Hegel (1770–1831), the greatest of the German idealist philosophers who followed Kant (maybe without properly understanding him). In Hegel's conception "Absolute Spirit" (who sounds very like God) is progressively working out the destiny of the world through human history.[10] That might suggest a cosmically parochial conception of God tied to the story of the human race and its vicissitudes on this planet.[11]

Hegel claimed, with typical self-confidence, to encompass Christianity *within* his enormous panorama of human development as an imagistic, nonliteral, popular presentation of the universal truths that his systematic philosophy aimed to express in logical, conceptual form. But his system has given rise to opposing interpretations ever since. One view steers away from pantheism toward more orthodox theism by interpreting "Absolute Spirit" as something or Someone *beyond* the universe, as well as being present in the evolutionary and historical processes within it. "Panentheism" is the usual label for the view that God is in some sense present in the whole of nature but also transcends it. How far that differs from the classic theology of the unchangeable nature of God depends on how to interpret the little word "in," when saying that God is present *in* nature.[12]

Pantheism dispenses with any idea of a transcendent purposive creator who loves us and acts to save us from ourselves. That is bad news to traditional believers, but it may be a tempting thought to those who want to save something from traditional theism without being committed to the whole package.

7

DEISM

The notion of divine action is central to the Bible: from beginning to end there is talk of God creating the world, speaking to people, causing floods and plagues and pregnancies, influencing minds, allowing or reversing the invasions of conquerors; and in the New Testament God is said to have acted for our salvation in the life, death, and resurrection of Jesus. In Islam the defining self-revelation of Allah is the "recitations" revealed to Muhammad and recorded in the Qur'an. These stories and pictures and doctrines have been recycled in Jewish and Christian and Muslim theology and worship down the centuries, and they remain vivid in many minds today. The common assumption has been that God acts in *some* events but not in others, or at least that he is active in them in a more specific manner than his general creative and providential care over everything.

But since the rise of Newtonian science in the seventeenth century, the idea of God intervening in the course of nature has been widely thought to be inconsistent with the scientific outlook. Miraculous divine acts have been understood as breaking the normal laws of nature (as we saw with Spinoza). Deism, in reaction, retains belief in a creator God who started everything off, but it holds that he does not act within the world thereafter.[1] Some deists may retain belief in the continuous sustaining activity of God, they just deny that he makes any special interventions in certain events rather than others.

The French Enlightenment thinker Voltaire (1694–1778) was typical of his century in this regard. He was a vituperate opponent of the Roman Catholic Church, but unlike his more radical atheist contemporaries he retained belief in a supreme divine being, though only on a deist understanding.[2] Deism was a widespread view in England in the eighteenth century and among the founding fathers of the American revolution including Thomas Paine, Benjamin Franklin, George Washington, Thomas Jefferson, and John Adams.[3] It is still an organized religious movement today.[4]

Adherents of the Abrahamic religions have usually maintained that God is the agent of events in the world, and yet that he is unchangeable "in himself." Harsh critics may dismiss this as a *reductio ad absurdum*—for how can God act at a specific time without undergoing some mental change at the time? Believers may reply that this is one of the mysteries that have to be accepted "on faith." But it is one thing to accept on faith a proposition that one can *understand*, though it is not justified by the evidence available[5]— for instance faith in a stranger's honesty, a company's profitability, or a spouse's fidelity. But it is something different to accept "on

faith" a putative "proposition" that one admits to be beyond all
possible evidence, perhaps even paradoxical.[6] The most fundamental questions about theological claims are not just about their
truth but also about their meaning, and, in the case at hand, we
are trying to understand what can be meant by saying that a transcendent, changeless God acts within the events of history.

Theologians try to fend off any impression of paradox or incoherence about the idea of God acting within the world, and a
variety of conceptions have been developed in response to this
problem. "Deism" is the label for views that retain belief in a creator (understood as benevolent) who brought the world into existence in the beginning but deny that he makes (or is even *able*
to make?) any particular interventions in its subsequent history.
The view can be characterized, crudely, as that God sets up the
world-machine in the first place but then leaves it to run entirely
by itself. In another picture he is likened to an absentee landlord
who buys a property and signs a lease but either cares nothing
for the consequences or is impotent to do anything about them.
In a third analogy he is likened to a playwright who writes an
outline of a plot but leaves it to the actors to improvise the play.
In such pictures conceptual difficulties about God's action are
reduced to his initial creation, avoiding any idea of him acting to
reveal himself through particular people, historical episodes, or
miraculous events. This offered an attractive compromise to some
early modern thinkers. If the creator leaves the world to follow
the natural laws that he set up, science can have the whole universe to itself as its unrivaled field—except perhaps the creation

itself (though big bang cosmology seems to offer a physical, non-theological account of that).

Many deists were especially fond of the argument from (or more precisely, *to*) design, namely inference from the characteristics of the living world to the existence of a divine creator. The manifest adaptation of species to their environments, the apparent "design-plan" in their structure and behavior, has long suggested to many the existence of a supreme divine designer (poetically expressed in the *Psalms* and at the end of the book of *Job*). William Paley made famous use of this argument in the first decade of the nineteenth century, but fifty years later Darwin's theory of natural selection in *The Origin of Species* blew it out of the water. We can still feel wonder at all those intricate and exquisite adaptations to environment, but the inference from them to the existence of a divine designer has collapsed in the face of the overwhelming scientific success of the theory of evolution of species by natural selection, modernized in the light of genetics, DNA, and the mathematical theory of populations.[7] Last-ditch efforts have been made by a few biologists committed to a fundamentalist interpretation of *Genesis* to identify some vestiges of "intelligent design," but they have not satisfied scientific and philosophical critics. A consistent deist will have to retreat to saying that God initially decreed the laws of nature, including the chemical structure of DNA that enables the copying of genes with occasional variations, and then left the whole course of evolution to run by itself.

In denying the literal truth of God's revelatory or redemptive intervention, deism parts company with mainstream traditional theism. Deists are not totally bereft of spirituality or ethics, however. They can worship their God. They can hardly go in for petitionary prayer, but they might see prayer as seeking God's will (asking what God wants us to do, rather than asking him to do things). They can appeal to the facts of human nature (biological, psychological, and social) and argue that God in his benevolent wisdom has intended us to evolve in the way we have. So our divinely created nature points us in the direction we need to go, and we should respect our creator by living in accordance with his design-plan, e.g. by devotedly caring for our children. But evolution only arranges for survival and reproduction, on average. That does not tell us how to spend the rest of our time. And why do we so often go *wrong*? Why do we like stuff that is bad for us, why does sexuality sometimes take perverse forms, and why do we kill each other individually and collectively? And what can be done about that? There is little in deism to explain human sinfulness, except the reflection that even a divinely foreseen process of evolution can only produce *more or less* adequate results from what has already existed in ancestral populations, and cannot guarantee perfect adaptation to changing circumstances, let alone moral perfection. Deist ethics can hardly amount to more than Spinozist mental reconciliation to natural necessity.

Deism has been characteristic of many scientifically minded yet residually theist thinkers. The issues around divine action still divide theologians. One recent holder of the Regius Chair of Divinity in the University of Oxford practically abandoned the idea of particular divine interventions in the world,[8] but his successor has defended a more robust traditional understanding of God's activity,[9] a topic we will discuss in the next chapter. Deism seems a rather unstable halfway house between traditional belief and atheism.

8

THE GOD WHO CHANGES
AND ACTS

Long ago Plato laid down a plausible condition for something to be *real*: that it has the power to affect other things, or be affected it-self.[1] By that criterion, for God to be real he must be able to make changes in the world or be affected by what happens (or both). The former belief has long been part of Judaism, Christianity, and Islam (though denied by deism), but whether events in the world can have *effects* on God to which he *reacts* in real time is a question on which theologians differ.

As we saw in Chapter 3, the classic medieval conception of God was of a necessary being who is "impassable," not subject to any kind of change. Some biblical passages suggest that God is change-less ("Before the mountains were brought forth or the earth and the world were born, from age to age you are God," *Psalm* 90:2). But other texts speak of God being angered by what people do (*Genesis* 6:11–13; *Exodus* 4:14; *Deuteronomy* 4:21), resolving to punish them and changing his mind (*Genesis* 8:21; *Exodus* 33:14; *Jeremiah* 18:8–10). Yet in direct contradiction to the latter, we read in *1 Samuel* 15:29 that "God who is the Splendor of Israel does not deceive, nor does he change his mind, as a mortal might do." The prophetic writings are overflowing with talk about God's interventions in the tangled and often violent history of ancient Israel. If read literally, such passages imply that God *is* affected by human events and acts in response to them.

According to theological tradition God is omniscient: he knows everything that there is to be known: all the physical facts of cosmology, geography, biology, and history, but also the inner secrets of our minds and hearts (*Psalm* 139; *Hebrews* 4:12–13)—though we are not told *how* he knows. Many theologians have assumed that in his omniscience God *foresees* everything that will happen. But if we have genuine freedom of will, then before a human decision is made there is no fact of the matter about which way it will go, and therefore no fact for anyone, not even the deity, to foresee.[2] So if there is any genuine human freedom, it seems that God has to wait to find out what we decide to do in each case, and is thus constantly acquiring *new* knowledge of the course of human affairs. God is also supposed to love us. So, does he suffer or get angry at each new episode of human folly and sinfulness, like an exasperated parent or schoolmaster? God may be necessary "in himself" (whatever that means), but it seems there must be much about him that is contingent on worldly circumstance.

God has also been traditionally thought of as the creator and sustainer of everything that happens, though that too seems to need some qualification in light of human free will. But even a limited divine potency suggests *some* ability to act within the world of time and space, to make a difference to what happens, particularly to people. If God is really to act shepherd-like to save me, he must know that I am in danger at the time, and he must be able to *do* something that will have the effect of rescuing me, in real time. The traditional belief has been that God can and does act within the world by miraculously suspending a law of nature, but for those who are not persuaded that determinism is true, or is a presupposition of science, there is the option of saying that God can influence aspects of events that are left undetermined by those laws.[3]

At this point we come to another dramatic fork in the theological road. One option is to maintain the classical tradition that God is not in time and does not go through a temporal series of perceptions, emotions, and actions.[4] According to this conception, he is eternal not in the sense of being everlasting, i.e., enduring through the whole of time, but rather of being tenseless, not immersed in time at all. In that respect he could be compared with mathematical objects such as numbers and geometrical figures, and with Platonic Forms—though unlike them he is supposed to be the creator and sustainer of the world and to be supremely good and loving.

But on the other theological option, God *does* genuinely persist through time, he goes through changes as he becomes aware of human events as they happen, and he acts in response to them. This divine temporality has been forthrightly embraced by a recent evangelical school of theology known as "open theism."[5] On this view God's knowledge of facts is constantly being extended by human decisions, he is affected by them, and he exerts his forgiveness and love to redeem humanity.[6] This conception has also been attractively developed by Keith Ward:

> [I]f the world is to be contingent, and man really free, contingency and mutability must exist within God himself.
>
> If genuinely free creatures are admitted, there is an overwhelmingly strong argument against Divine immutability and for Divine temporality.
>
> So the requirements of rational theology, seeking to explain the world in terms of the principle of sufficient reason, seeking an ideal form of explanation which would leave absolutely nothing unexplained, lead to irreconcilable conflict with the doctrine of creation, of Divine and creaturely freedom and contingency.[7]

A classic move in medieval theology was to allow for the acts of an eternal God in a changing world by distinguishing between God as the single "primary" cause of everything that happens and the manifold "secondary" causes in the world, including human choices and actions. For example, the statement "God has given me a child" can be meant in two ways. One is to acknowledge that the normal course of conception, gestation, and birth (whose biological details and dangers are unknown to most of us who are not medics) has resulted in a child, where the God-bit simply expresses gratitude for the successful outcome of that delicate process. (It has to be admitted, however, that not every child is a wanted child. "God has given me a cancer" can be meant either in acceptance of God's perceived will or in bitter complaint against it.) In the other interpretation of "God has given me a child" there is a claim that God has intervened miraculously in a way that cannot be explained by medical science and even involves breaking the laws of biology.[8] The combination of God as "primary" (sustaining) cause of everything, with "secondary" causes operating in all the ways that empirical science can study, does not imply the possibility of miracles. But it does not exclude it either: if God is credited with the power to intervene (as a "tertiary" cause?) where he judges it good to do so, readers of the Bible and the Qur'an can take quite literally the passages in which God is represented as doing just that.

God has been said in some theological tradition to "concur" in every human action, i.e., to be one among the various causal factors that make our actions possible, that whenever we do something (for better or for worse), God in some arcane sense acts with us.[9] That would seem to make him at least partially responsible for our evil deeds. The twentieth-century Anglican theologian Austin

Farrer embraced what he called "the paradox of double agency, in which every event has both natural and divine causes."[10] But if the idea is that God sets up the world in the first place and then leaves it to run (and run amok when human beings get to work), that takes us back to deism. If the claim is that in some sense God is the concurrent agent behind every event, that seems to imply that everything that happens is God's will, or is at least *permitted* by him, even in cases of extreme natural disaster or human malevolence which he surely *could* have intervened to prevent or ameliorate. If on the other hand it is said that God is the agent only of *some* events within history, we are faced with the questions of how to distinguish these from the rest, and of why he acts there and not elsewhere.

Ward says repeatedly that it is difficult or impossible to know in which cases God acts.[11] Yet elsewhere in the same book he declares that "it should be quite possible in principle to know what sort of thing an act of God is, and to distinguish various sorts of such action both from the exercise of the powers of natural objects and from free creaturely acts." He says that in the witness of the Bible "we possess here an impressive testimony to discerned acts of God in particular historical events."[12] But the confidence with which the biblical prophets interpreted the actions of God in the long-vanished history of ancient Israel does not give us guidance how to distinguish them in our time. Of course, Christianity believes in a once-and-for-all action of God in the birth, life, and death of Jesus. But can anyone identify with certainty, or even with any confidence, any particular act of God in post-biblical history? It is tempting to suggest that the discernment of divine action is not like the inquiries of detectives, judges, or historians into the activities of criminals, bureaucracies, or politicians, but more like the recognition of flashes of genius in literary or musical compositions, or steps of ethical progress in nations or cultures. But those are judgments of *value* rather than factual hypotheses about elusive supernatural machinations behind the scenes.

The belief that God *can* intervene in human affairs notoriously gives rise to the long-standing problem of evil: Why does he not prevent the manifold suffering in the world or at least alleviate it? The classic defense is to suggest that God may have long-term benevolent purposes that are inscrutable to us, totally beyond our understanding and knowledge, so that even what seem to us horrendous evils can be redeemed by God's control of the whole picture through time and space. That is to admit, like Job when he is finally confronted by God himself, that we human beings cannot understand why God allows so much suffering, whether from natural causes, malice, or negligence. But that position is open to the complaint of Dostoyevsky's Ivan Karamazov that the torture of a single child (let alone the genocide of millions) cannot be redeemed by any theory about the overall divinely ordained goodness of the whole show.[13]

It seems that neither theist nor atheist can answer the heart-wrung question "Why did this happen to *me?*" (Wasn't the Lord supposed to care for me like a shepherd?) except in purely causal scientific terms, which do not speak to the human predicament. Neither believers nor nonbelievers can supply any existentially satisfying account, any *reason* rather than a cause, why accidents, deprivation, and disease happen to particular people. Some theists may find comfort in the thought that God may have an unknowable purpose behind their suffering, but others will feel like protesting (as Job did to his would-he comforters) that it is unfair, unredeemed, unjustified. Unbelievers also divide into those who may manage to accept their suffering as part of the overall scheme of things and those who see it as desperately unlucky, though not unfair, because there is no question of fairness about such events.

There remains an element of human freedom in almost all theology,[14] but it is most explicitly recognized in open theism, which has accordingly been called "free will theism." God's forgiving love, his redemption in Christ, or his self-revelation in the Qur'an, is said to be offered to everyone, but it is up to each individual whether to receive it, so there is no guarantee of individual salvation or of overall progress in society. The three millennia of Judaism, the two millennia of Christianity, and the millennium and a half of Islam have produced only mixed and unstable results—that has to be agreed. Nevertheless, it has been a central feature of these Abrahamic religions to see divine meaning and purpose within and behind the ambiguous course of human history, in which good and bad appear intertwined, writhing together and multiplying like snakes. There was some plausibility in the postulation of rival good and evil powers by ancient Manicheism, but monotheists have always thought of God as ultimately sovereign (though some have personified evil in the figure of Satan). Monotheists have seen his creation as fundamentally good and as destined eventually to reach a divinely ordained happy ending in heaven, though the ride is bumpy and some people may end up in a less salubrious place.

Enlightenment philosophers, such as Kant, took up the theme of progress in human history, usually in a more secular interpretation. And the advent of evolutionary theory widened the nineteenth-century belief in progress to include the deep past of all life on earth. There have been explicitly atheist theories of progress: notably Marx's materialist theory of history that turned Hegel's idealism on its head by asserting that material and economic factors are the real driving force behind all human development.[15] In the early twentieth century, Teilhard de Chardin (1881–1955), a French geologist, paleontologist, and unorthodox Jesuit, offered a hybrid biological-theological conception of progress which represented God as waiting for the consummation of human history in Christ.[16] Teilhard saw the cosmic Christ as an attractive force drawing all events toward God's loving destiny (obviously this was meant to be a spiritual rather than physical force). This speculative combination of evolution with theology has been found congenial by some (there are Teilhard Societies), but it has been criticized from both scientific and theological sides.[17]

The central assertion of open theism, that God changes, continues to divide theologians.[18] Most theological disagreements still tend to be expressed in the idiom of rival statements about the nature of God, i.e., about some objective, human-independent, ultimate metaphysical fact of the matter. But there seems to be no agreed method to resolve such theological disputes: philosophical reasoning does not settle them, nor does science or historical inquiry.[19] Typical of most theologians is William Hasker when in his contribution to *The Openness of God* he makes confidently realist claims about the nature of God.[20] But he is less typical and to my mind more realistic about the nature of his discipline in concluding:

> It is in the end out of the question for anyone to "prove"
> that a particular conception of God is the correct one.
> Rather, one simply finds that a particular way of understanding the things of God makes the most sense, and
> provides the greatest illumination, in the overall context
> of one's thinking and living.[21]

One way of defusing the clash between eternal and temporal conceptions of God would be to interpret the latter as *applications* of general, eternally true, theological statements. "God forgives those who truly repent" can be pastorally applied to particular people and times, e.g., "If you, Jane Doe, truly repent of what you did last week, God will forgive you." We might say that God is eternal in the sense that he has permanent dispositions to love and forgiveness, yet he exerts his love and forgiveness on particular individuals as human history unfolds. We might thus give sense to the thought that his existence or "essence" is necessary but his "energies" vary over time. A more radically reductive interpretation would be that theological statements should be understood as recognitions of unchanging, ultimate *values*, rather misleadingly cast in ontological mode as claims about metaphysical *facts*.

Unsympathetic critics may conclude that on this issue, as on others, the concept of God is subject to such severe internal tensions that it collapses into incoherence. We have noted flat disagreements on whether God is a person, on whether beliefs about him need support by evidence, whether he is simple, and on whether he changes and acts. Let us inquire in Part II whether such questions merely reflect choices between alternative forms of language or conceptual schemes.

PART II
WORDS

The second half of the twentieth century saw considerable attention to religious language, its meaning, its expressive use, and its
social setting in ways of life. In Part I we have already encountered
the suggestion that the word "God" should not be interpreted as
the name of a particular person or being or spirit, even if as a
matter of sociological fact millions of religious believers have understood it that way. Perhaps most atheists and agnostics have also
taken it thus, as the conception they *reject*. But in theology (as in
science, and in the humanities) it is possible to argue that popular
usage and commonsense conceptions are ambiguous, misleading,
or downright mistaken. Some theologians have not been afraid to
say so.

INSTRUMENTALISM

If we review widespread uses of the G-word in contemporary society we find a variety of expressions that need not express any serious religious commitment or theological belief. People squeal "Oh my God!" merely to express surprise, whether pleasant or unpleasant. Old-fashioned insurance policies excluded cover for "acts of God," presumably meaning any natural disaster that could not reasonably be foreseen: the insurance companies hardly meant to get involved in theological arguments about God's action in the world! The driver who sees the car in front of him stopped for speeding may say, "There but for the grace of God go I," meaning that it was a matter of sheer luck he was not caught, but he probably does not have a theology of divine grace. Our cultural heritage extending back two or three millennia has left these fossilized phrases in our language, but like fossils they are not alive. An Australian cartoonist reported the following interchange between his parents: "Where in God's name is the bloody hammer?—God only knows," and says he came to regard "God" as a one-word poem.[1] It seems we tend to invoke the G-poem when we meet with difficulty, un-solved mystery, or even a nice surprise.

Moving to religious language that is *supposed* to be taken more seriously (but often is not), consider rituals such as grace before meals; prayers in synagogues, churches, or mosques; and religious festivals and rites of passages such as Passover, bar-mitzvahs, Ramadan, harvest festivals, Easter rituals, baptisms, weddings, and funerals. Traditional formulas are used, and the name of God will usually be invoked, but it is easy to hear and repeat the ritual words without thinking about their meaning. Such speech-acts are often performed because they are "the done thing," time-honored formulas for the seasons and events in life. They also tend to func-tion as identity-proclaiming badges of ethnic community (though thereby providing grounds of difference that can harden into isola-tion, intolerance, or conflict). Not much in the way of theological belief (or even ethics) may be involved for many participants, but such rituals *can* be part of a genuinely religiously inspired form of life. And there are many gradations of clarity, sincerity, and belief involved: human psychology and sociology are untidy.

One way of understanding religious language recognizes *only* its expressivist aspects and ritualistic uses, leaving out any objec-tive reference and truth-claims. It is widely accepted, of course, that religious ways of life involve *more* than propositional belief. Living faith involves *attitudes* and *practices*, such as reverence, wor-ship, gratitude, prayer, a sense of failure and sinfulness, confes-sion, repentance, forgiveness and spiritual renewal, the reception of sacraments, celebration of marriages and births, mourning the dead, a sense of social solidarity, hope and resolve for the future. All that is surely true, but the controversial "instrumentalist" interpretation of religion is that even those who take their religious practice seriously do not need to think of it as focusing on God conceived of as a supernatural person or even as any sort of transcendent reality. The language for worship, prayer, and ritual may remain replete with God-talk, but the suggestion is that one can "go along with" it in practice and derive some sort of spiritual benefit from doing so, while not understanding it as having any objective reference or truth.

This presents a radical challenge to traditional theological understanding. It goes beyond the thought (familiar to readers by now) that God is not a person or a particular being: the claim would be that the G-word need not be interpreted as denoting any sort of human-independent reality. Such a denial can take various forms, the most trenchant of which is that the use of theological language need not have *any* sort of reference at all but consists only in the utterance of verbal formulas whose repeated usage has practical effects on their users. (It is often assumed that the effects are desirable, though cynics might question that.) This can be called "instrumentalism" since it interprets religious speech-acts (and silent prayers involving religious concepts) as mere means or instruments toward certain independently identifiable human ends. It seems to compare religious language to "spells": the utterance of verbal formulas, which may be in an unknown language, but which are supposed to have magical effects, as in the Harry Potter stories that have resurrected the notion of spells in popular culture.

To move nearer to religious practice, consider the use of "mantras"—words or phrases suggested to a novice by adepts of a meditative or devotional tradition. Mantras may be personalized or may have a general usage, but the recommendation is to utter or think them repeatedly, with the assurance that one can thus make progress on the spiritual path. Some Christian spiritual direction has encouraged the repeated incantatory use of prayers such as the Jesus prayer "Lord Jesus, have mercy on me, a sinner." In that case it is implausible to suggest that the meaning of the words does not matter, for they imply recognition of one's own unworthiness judged by a divine standard associated with Jesus of Nazareth, together with hope of forgiveness from that divine source. The spiritual effect of *those* words is surely connected with their cognitive meaning.

The accommodation with Anglican Christianity suggested by R. B. Braithwaite, a distinguished philosopher of science in Cambridge in the 1950s, was frankly instrumentalist.[2] His proposal allowed him to take part in services in the college chapel while interpreting the words as expressing an *agapeistic* (universally loving) way of life, and hearing biblical stories as stimulus to that commitment. That involved *understanding* the stories of course, though not necessarily as historical records. But when it came to the creed, was he perhaps prepared to *sing* it but not to *say* it? Singing could be understood as a harmless ritual that might even be beneficial, but saying it sounds like the expression of belief in claims that the philosopher's intellectual conscience might strain at. On reflection though, it is perfectly possible to say things without believing the relevant propositions—when lying, acting, quoting, speaking in absence of mind, or perhaps in ritual. Presumably even the sacraments can be received in an instrumentalist spirit, as a reverent ritual that may have good effects.

Perhaps many occupants of pews or synagogues or mosques, if questioned closely, might find themselves in a similar position. And it is not dishonorable to participate in traditional rites only because one believes they help maintain oneself and one's community in a good way of life. But many believers and most theologians will surely say that is to miss out on the dimension of religion that involves some sort of claim to reference and truth. It is surely only because of *doubts* about theological meaning or truth that some people are inclined to instrumentalism.

10

REDUCTIONISM

If instrumentalism offers an expressive but non-factual use of theistic language, reductionism proposes that it *can* have factual meaning but only in an implicit concealed way, about human rather than transcendent states of affairs. The classic statement of this approach was by Ludwig Feuerbach (1804–1872) in his book *The Essence of Christianity*, in which he remorselessly tried to reinterpret all the concepts of Christianity in humanist terms.[1] Describing himself as "nothing but a natural philosopher in the domain of mind" (i.e., he was setting out to be a scientific psychologist), his guiding idea was that "religion itself . . . believes in nothing else than the truth and divinity of human nature" (xiv, xvi), so "the true sense of Theology is Anthropology" (xvii, 54, 58, 339).

But what then is human nature, to which theology supposedly reduces? Feuerbach followed philosophical tradition in listing three basic mental faculties: reason, will, and affection (i.e., feeling or emotion). It is a peculiarity of humans as distinct from other animals that we are aware of our own limitations, our unworthiness, and indeed our mortality: but Feuerbach says this is "only because the perfection, the infinitude of his species, is perceived by him, whether as an object of feeling, of conscience, or of the thinking consciousness" (presumably he meant that we have an *ideal* of perfection by which to judge ourselves). "As far as thy nature reaches, so far reaches thy unlimited self-consciousness, so far art thou God." If feeling is the essential organ of religion, "the nature of God is nothing else than an expression of the nature of feeling," and consciousness of God is nothing other than the self-consciousness of human beings (7–9).

Feuerbach says that most people's ignorance of this reductive identity is "fundamental to the peculiar nature of religion," though it is "evident to the thinker, by whom religion is viewed objectively." So for him religious belief involves for unenlightened people an *illusion* of reference to something transcendent. But once we have seen through the illusion (as is supposed to happen when we read Feuerbach or his successors Durkheim and Freud), we can continue to use the religious language with its purely human meaning about our highest values, what we aspire to be. The divine being "is nothing else than the human being, or rather, the human nature purified, freed from the limits of the individual man." So for Feuerbach God is not human nature as it is, but an ideal of what we can be and *ought* to be: "the divine love is only human love made objective, affirming itself" (13–4, 29–30, 35–6, 46, 55–6).

Feuerbach's case was enthusiastically endorsed by Marx and Marxists, though they tended to emphasize the crusading atheistic bits rather than his positive talk of Love with a capital "L." The influential German liberal theologian Friedrich Schleiermacher (1768–1834), in tune with the romantic movement of the early nineteenth century, agreed with Feuerbach's emphasis on the fundamental importance of feeling in religion but managed to stay within the orbit of Christian theism (if only just, according to some theologians).

There have been many recent versions of the reductionist view that all talk of God should be reconstrued in humanistic terms. A prominent example is the Cambridge philosopher of religion Don Cupitt's claim that God is a symbol standing for "the religious imperative" that "commands us to become free spirits," which we "autonomously adopt and impose on ourselves." In other words, God is "what the religious requirement comes to mean to us as we respond to it."[2] In a later book Cupitt defined God as "the sum of our values, representing to us their ideal unity, their claims upon us and their creative power."[3] God is thus understood as a personification of our values, rather in the way that artists or sculptors in bygone eras personified virtues as human figures (usually of buxom female form).[4] Cupitt affirmed Feuerbachian reductionism when he asked: Is "God is love" fully and straightforwardly convertible with "Love is God"? and baldly answered: Yes.[5] (These quotations are from the earlier phase of his output of books proposing a non-realist revolution (or perpetual revolution?) in religion, displaying a prodigious intellectual appetite and a seemingly effortless flow of words. I will examine themes from his later work in the next chapter.)

But if the *word* "God" is a mere fossil for many people in our secularized societies, maybe some *sentences* containing it, such as "God forgives those who truly repent," need not be. That may express something existentially and communally important, which can *perhaps* be equally expressed (though less pithily) in humanist terms: if one realizes that one has done something wrong, one can stop blaming oneself if one apologizes and does one's best to restore the relationship with the person one has wronged, and resume one's place in family and community. Psychotherapy and social psychology can surely provide an extra depth of understanding of the psychological processes involved. I will return to this topic in Part III.

There are some peculiar nouns in the English language that do not refer to anything in particular yet contribute to the meaning of sentences containing them. Consider the word "sake," as in "I brought it for Mary's sake," which is equivalent to "I brought it in order to benefit Mary in some way," and is not to be construed on the model of "I brought it for Mary's cake," where her cake is an independently identifiable material object. Underneath linguistic parallels there can be big differences in meaning, as Wittgenstein and his successors in twentieth-century "ordinary language philosophy" took delight in pointing out. Cakes can be baked, admired, and consumed, but one can't do *anything* with "a sake"—indeed it is improper to talk of *a* sake or of sakes in the plural.[6] However this is not to suggest that the G-word is as superfluous as "sake," for the latter seems to be an isolated oddity of English idiom that could surely be dropped from our vocabulary without loss of expressive power, and there may no one-word synonym in other languages.[7]

So is theology really reducible to ethics, or to the meaning we find (or construct) in our lives? If there are humanist equivalents to sentences such as "God forgives those who truly repent," why bother with the theological versions? Are they an optional extra, adding a flavoring that is attractive to those with a taste for such cultural "fossils," but which others find repellent? Is God in danger of being reduced to a mere figure of speech, even if rather more ancient, venerable, and versatile than "sake"? Can't we "do" spirituality without "doing" God? A lot of people want to, these days.

There are different interpretations of the reductionist program, however. The most ambitious version would be to find a humanist equivalent for *every* theological sentence that Christian tradition has taken seriously, as Feuerbach set out to do. I have tentatively suggested only one putative equivalence above. To do the same for *all* talk of God would be a very big ask, and disagreements will quickly break out over what is equivalent to what.

Another version of the program would be to propose nontheist equivalents (or partial interpretations) of such Christian (or other religious) claims as lend themselves to such treatment, and to dismiss the rest as unnecessary, or even incoherent. That would *not* be to treat theist and nontheist language impartially as equal alternatives, it would be to try to interpret a portion of Christian talk in nontheist terms. And partiality could go the other way: theologians may want to recast ethical, psychothera-peutic, or new-age-spiritual talk in theist terms and argue that an important dimension is missing if God is left out.

11

POSTMODERNISM

In recent years there has emerged a yet more radical strand of non-realism about God that derives from a very bold philosophical thesis variously labeled "linguistic idealism," "constructivism," or "postmodernism," namely that the language we use in some sense *creates* the world we inhabit. This has roots in the philosophy of Kant, in a tempting (but disputable) interpretation of his "Copernican revolution in metaphysics" and his elusive doctrine of "transcendental idealism."[1] The theme of revolutionary human relativity and creativity was expressed more aggressively in the writings of Nietzsche and has been further developed by a variety of twentieth-century continental philosophers. It has been applied not just to religion but also to *all* language on any subject matter.

The later writings of Don Cupitt contain increasingly extreme statements of such linguistic idealism and its supposed implications for a total revolution in religion: "We have come to see that there can be for us nothing but the worlds that are constituted for us by our own language and activities. All meaning and truth and value are man-made and could not be otherwise." And, "The world has gradually turned into a changing human cultural construction."[2] That last statement is carelessly worded: his point is surely not that the world has turned into a cultural construction, but that we have recently *come to realize* that that (supposedly!) is all the world is and ever has been.

Nevertheless, it is ludicrously false to say that the world is literally a human construction. We have to agree on reflection that our changing *conceptions* of the world involve our cultural constructions—but if that is all that is meant, it takes much of the sting out of linguistic idealism. For that surely presupposes that the physical and biological world (the sun and this planet, the volcanos and oceans, the dinosaurs and Neanderthals) all preexisted human beings, our languages, and our cultural constructions. Another provocative Cupittian saying suffers from the same ambiguity: "The very large and slightly absurd object that physicists call the Universe can only be produced if the life-world is already first given."[3] But physicists (who themselves have to be trained in a life-world, from childhood up to doing PhDs in the scientific life-world) can only produce *theories* about the universe: not even the most overweening of them would claim to produce the *universe* itself!

In one place Cupitt rows back a little from extreme non-realism: "The suggestion that the idea of God is man-made would only seem startling if we could point by contrast to something that had not been made by men. . . . God is man-made only in the non-startling sense that everything is."[4] But that invites the riposte of robust common sense that lots of stuff is definitely not man-made—for example the stars, Jupiter, the Falkland Islands, chimpanzees, gold, oak trees, water, oxygen, and the DNA within us. If God can be considered as real in his *own* way (whatever that is) as all those material things are in *their* ways, he has nothing to fear from this philosophy.

Postmodernists will reply that our *ideas* or *concepts* of God are man-made, like all ideas or concepts. But that cries out for clarification of in what sense they are "man-made." To be sure the *words* are man-made, for there are different words in different languages for the same things, multiple linguistic conventions that have grown up within past communities without any meetings or "conventions" to legislate for them. But the stuff in the physical world that is *referred to* in the above examples is not man-made, and the references of the relevant words are fixed primarily by perceptual encounter with the relevant objects, or instances of those natural kinds. With those words, at least, their meaning— the idea or concept they convey—is at least partly determined by what there is in the world.[5] Most certainly, the existence and nature of what those words refer to is independent of the mental and verbal gymnastics of human beings. That basic sort of realism is undeniable.

Linguistic idealism has been fashionable in some intellectual circles, in which perhaps Cupitt spent too much time and has allowed himself to be led into denying the obvious.[6] But even that famous high priest of postmodern "deconstruction" Jacques Derrida repudiated the absurd view (often attributed to him) that

nothing exists outside texts.[7] After all, humans came into existence as a species and as individuals before we could *produce* any
texts.[8]

Besides, linguistic idealism, if fully thought through, has
to apply to the *self* and to *human nature*, just as much as to the
world and God. The claim that *we* create reality through our use
of language suggests that "we"—members of our various linguistic and cultural communities—must have some determinate
nature if we are to perform any such mysterious acts of creation.
Feuerbach himself assumed that there is a human "essence," a set
of basic general facts about human nature, in terms of which theological language can be redefined. But many thinkers, not just
postmodernists, have denied that there is any fixed human essence
and have asserted instead that human nature varies across cultures
and historical change. Marx was a prime example, though even
he had to assume some biologically given human nature, if only
our need to eat a certain range of foodstuffs and to reproduce via
a long period of childhood dependence. But the character of any
human individual is at least partly a creation of his or her culture,
and individual characters may change when social circumstances
change or perhaps when someone undergoes a Sartrean "radical
conversion," so there is some truth in the saying that there is no
fixed and abiding "self."

Despite what has been overconfidently claimed about the
philosophically tricky relation between language and reality, it
remains open for theists to say that although *ideas* of God vary con-
siderably (as this inquiry shows) and are in some sense man-made,

God himself is not a cultural construction, and his existence
and his nature do not depend on human beings. In mathematics
new concepts have been constructed (or discovered?) over the
centuries, and new theorems are still being proved. Even if we
take the non-Platonic view that mathematical objects do not exist
independently of our minds, we still have to acknowledge that
whether a result has been proved is a mind-independent matter
(though suitably qualified minds have to make a judgment when
they referee a paper for a journal). There can be objectivity of
truth without material existence. So we still have to see if any sort
of realist understanding of God can be explained and defended.
An alleged obstacle has been removed, but a positive case still
needs to be made.

12

RELATIVISM

A subtly different approach to religious language involves a relativist philosophy according to which there are alternative "language-games," practices, "forms of life," or conceptual schemes. This theme has been prominent in neo-Wittgensteinian philosophy of religion and in anthropology.[1] It is claimed that we cannot talk of equivalence or reducibility (or even of incompatibility or contradiction) between statements from different conceptual schemes. Within a given language-game there are rules about what can meaningfully or truly be said, but the typical relativist claim is that between two systems there is no common or neutral ground on which any sort of rational comparison or evaluation can be made. Devotees of each will say "this is the way *we* do things; this is the sort of thing *we* say in this situation"; but for anyone who stands outside the relevant community, there is no test by which one practice or system can be said to be any more rational or true than another. So there can be no appeal to "reality" (objective, neutral, unconceptualized reality,

"things as they are in themselves") to decide between conceptual schemes. About each, one can only say (with Wittgenstein),
"This language-game is played—that is an anthropological fact."
And the relativist implication is that if you're not in the business
of playing that game, you have no right to criticize it, you must
respectfully leave it as it is.

In light of this, it may be tempting to think that we can treat
theist and ethical-cum-therapeutic terminology (perhaps with a
dash of new age spirituality) as alternative conceptual schemes,
each of them found comfortable and useful by a certain section of
the population, which may help their users to live ethical, fulfilled
and meaningful lives, but between which there can be no neutral arbitration. They would be seen simply as alternative linguistic
systems, with no call for dispute or discrimination. The case might
be compared to that of *languages* proper: it is difficult to argue that
English is better overall than French or Chinese or Swahili—they
are just different.

In this would-be tolerant, multicultural spirit many people
now tend to say that this clinical abstention from evaluation must
be extended to all the various *religions* of the world, since each
involves a different language-game, ritual, and form of life with
its own peculiar but uncriticizable rules. That is to claim not
merely that toleration of other religions as anthropological facts
on the ground is pragmatically advisable in interfaith relations and
in social and political policy: it is to assert that criticism of one
religion from the standpoint of another makes no sense, it is *con-
ceptually* as well as politically incorrect.

But there is a general ground for doubt about this relativist philosophy. For it rests on the assumption that there are clear distinctions between language-games, conceptual schemes, and religious ways of life, so that we can always tell *which* system a given sentence or speech-act or religious practice belongs to. But are religion and science completely separate systems, as such theorizing assumes? The continuing controversies about Darwinian evolution and about the supposedly purposive fine-tuning of the physical constants suggest otherwise. And what about the various *sciences*: are physics and biology, archeology, and linguistics in different systems or are they part of one big scientific system? Within Christianity, do Orthodox, Catholics, and Protestants speak and think and live in different systems or in rival versions of the same system? Are Sunni and Shia Islam two religions or one? Are religion and ethics different systems? And what about psychoanalysis, psychotherapy, or fashionable Westernized Buddhist spirituality? The notions of a language-game, a form of life, or a conceptual system are not precise technical terms; they are too vague to do any serious philosophical work, for we lack any clear criterion of identity by which to distinguish conceptual schemes. Within and between the sciences and religions, ethics and therapies there are no strict boundary lines across which understanding, dispute, and criticism are impossible. A generalized relativism is a lazy philosophy.

But that does not license us to rest complacently within our inherited or adopted religious faith, ideology, or worldview. Most of us have a large set of beliefs that may be roughly subdivided into mathematical, scientific, and historical knowledge, facts about ourselves and our acquaintances, plus ethical, political, and aesthetic values or beliefs, and (in some people) theological creeds.[2] If there are strains and tensions between some of our beliefs, there is a rational requirement (which many people find it convenient to ignore) to achieve reconciliation and consistency by reinterpreting or even abandoning some of our beliefs. When we encounter differences from what others affirm, there is a challenge to our understandings to which many people may not rise (and to which it may sometimes be politic *not* to rise), but it is there to be pondered by anyone with the inclination, the ability, and the requisite sensitivity.

Given the connections (and distinctions) between theological and ethical/humanist/psychological accounts of human life, I recommend a continuing dialogue, to explore with patience and mutual respect how far each can be accommodated within the other, and what differences may remain.[3] All sides may learn something from the process, provided they are prepared to move out of their comfort zone and admit that their view may not encompass all the truth and may even contain some errors. This is not to say that religion can be reduced entirely to ethics. It is to allow that theological language (or some of it) may have a role that is more than the expression of human attitudes and may involve some kind of truth-claim about wider reality. But in view of the controversies down the centuries, such a conclusion has still to be earned.[4]

13

WITTGENSTEINIAN CHRISTIANITY

Much relativist thinking in the twentieth century has been inspired by the later philosophy of Wittgenstein in which he introduced his seductive but vague notions of language-games and forms of life (though he can hardly be held responsible for the views of his followers). A radically Wittgensteinian interpretation of Christianity has been offered by Gareth Moore whose work is not as well-known as that of the Welsh philosopher D. Z. Phillips, a tireless producer of books interpreting religion in the neo-Wittgensteinian vein.[1] I suggest we can learn from some detailed attention to Moore's book, which is much less piously conventional than its title *Believing in God*.[2]

As we would expect from a member of the Dominican Order,[3] Moore is far from denying the reality of God. He affirms that God really exists, but he is concerned to elucidate what that means and does *not* mean. So he undertakes a program of careful, even nitpicking, work to show how, in his view, language about God is actually used by Christian believers. He reiterates the theme we have already encountered that "God" is *not* the name of something or somebody, not even a heavenly spiritual thing or person (18, 44–6, 61–2, 280, 284).[4] More positively he says: "we can establish the presence of the heavenly, spiritual God . . . by seeing an earthly, material man saying his prayers, *and nothing else*" (62, 188–9). That sounds very reductionist, seeming to define the presence of God in terms of a certain kind of human activity. Perhaps Moore means that sincere prayer brings a person *into* the presence of God; but an atheist can hear someone uttering prayers addressed to a deity (and be convinced of their sincerity) without being himself committed to the reality of God. It is only believers who will say that prayer establishes the presence of God.

Moore acknowledges that people can have vivid experiences of the presence of God, e.g., when praying or in great danger, and that these need not be illusory. But he insists they are not to be understood as experiences of a thing or person or spiritual being called "God" (64–7)—which invites the question how they *should* be understood. He later suggests that "what makes an experience a spiritual one is the way it is reacted to" (78), but that again suggests a reduction of the spiritual to a certain kind of human behavior, which is surely not his intention. Yet in some of what Moore says, attitudes toward God seem to be definable in humanistic terms: "Loving our neighbor is a condition of loving God, or is even what loving God *consists in*" (113; my italics); and "to fear God . . . is *not to fear at all*" (117).

As for God's action, Moore seems to tend again toward reductionism. He says God is real, though not in the way that human persons are real, and "it is not yet settled what it is for God to create and to act, to give rewards, to punish, to forgive, to give rain, to inspire virtue" (101). To say, "God has helped me" is "not an explanation of how you got through; it is an expression of the *mystery* of how you . . . did get through, *without help*" (133). "If I ask God for something, and get it, there is no further doubt . . . as to whether God gave it to me," "the question of agency does not arise" (204–5). If *anything* happens, it follows that God has brought it about,[5] but Moore repeatedly emphasizes that God is not an additional supernatural agent over and above human agents (212–3, 232, 235, 237–8, 249, 262, 268–9). He makes it sound as if saying that God brought something about is only to say that it happened, and praying to God for something amounts to no more than expressing a wish or hope.

Nevertheless, I think that Moore does not intend a Feuerbachian[6] reduction of all theistic language to human terms, but is insisting that it is only *in the context* of human religious experience and practice that Christian usage and belief can be understood. "It is not that belief in God . . . is somehow given an independent, theoretical meaning, and that we are then exhorted to develop the attitudes appropriate to such a being . . . the attitudes, dispositions and activities . . . are what give *sense* to our belief in God and what we believe about him" (147, 181). So a religion is part of a form of life, not a theory but a practice. A more cautious formulation would be that it is not *merely* or *primarily* a set of propositional beliefs but involves a way of life.

Does this imply a relativist view that no reason can be given for going for a particular religion rather than another—or none? Some of what Moore writes suggests that Christianity is merely one alternative amongst others. He says that "the question whether God exists is not a factual question . . . it is a question whether to adopt the concept 'God' . . . into the language, or to retain it" (39). "We use the concepts we use and not the concepts other societies use . . . we are *determined* to treat certain utterances in the way we do treat them, and not in the way the other society treats them. It is a rejection of their way of life" (73, 131, 226). The most explicit suggestion of relativism comes in Moore's "Unconcluding Remarks," where he imagines an African tribe who worship an idol made of wood and suggests that if he were enculturated into such a tribe, perhaps by marrying one of them (a nice fantasy for a Dominican friar!), he would come to share their way of life and would become "engaged in their religious life, with all its expressions in world and action" (286–7).[7]

The last line of the book is especially provocative: "people do not discover religious truths, they make them." That may suggest Cupittian linguistic idealism, but I do not think that Moore really means it, any more than reductionism or full-blown relativism. As a member of a Catholic religious order he surely believes that Christianity is true, or at least *better* than any alternative. But it is not clear how he can reconcile that with his relativist-sounding remarks. His imagined acculturation into an African tribe is ambiguous: Is he merely predicting that if he were to join such a tribe then as a matter of fact he would come to share their practices and beliefs, or is he asserting a relativist thesis that there can be no comparison in terms of rationality, truth, or ethics between his Christian way of life and the exotic one? Or does he after all believe that the former is better, on the most important dimensions of assessment?

Early in the book Moore appeals to ecclesiastical authority: "the argument of the orthodox may have to come down to saying 'This is just what the Christian faith is. This is what is said. This is what is believed and is to be believed. Believe this, not that'" (32). This too can be read in more than one way: the authority might consist merely in knowledge of the rules of a game or practice (whether chess, rugby, or the Dominican Order), and if so, the injunction is only about what to do and say *if* you want to join in that particular practice. But "authority" as Moore describes it sounds more like a *recommendation* of Christianity (or the authority's version of it) as better than any alternative.

Confirmation of this comes in the chapter where he expounds some of the teachings of Jesus, for example the reversal of worldly standards of greatness at *Luke* 22:26–7: "Let the greatest among you be like the youngest, and the leader like one who serves. For who is greater, he who reclines at dinner or he who serves? Is it not he who reclines? But I am in your midst as one who serves." Moore comments:

> *The disciples have to learn this new and paradoxical way*
> *of speaking as part of learning a new way of life. What*
> *is going on here is* not an arbitrary game *being played*

> *with language, an inconsequential joke, but is more akin*
> *to a linguistic change one may feel impelled to make as*
> *one may feel impelled to change one's way of life. (180;*
> *my italics)*

And this "feeling impelled" is not merely a physiological or emotional reaction, like an urge to scratch one's nose or to utter a rude remark, but involves some sort of *judgment* that a certain way of life is appropriate, good, or right. Moore says:

> *Our religious beliefs and language [he obviously means*
> *Christian beliefs and language] have their place within*
> *the context of a particular kind of human life, a life in*
> *which gratitude, generosity, lack of self-seeking, a sense*
> *of dependence and mystery, among other things, play an*
> *important, even a defining part. (147–8)*

But once again ambiguity resides in that phrase "have their place within." It could be read in a reductionist way, implying that Christian beliefs can be defined in terms of such a list of admirable human qualities. It could be taken as saying that a way of life informed by Christian belief and language will in fact display those qualities or *ought* to display them (even if not all those who profess the label "Christian" live up to that high standard). That leaves it open that lives inspired by other religions or by none might display those qualities too; in which case explicit commitment to Christian belief and ritual practice will be neither a sufficient nor a necessary condition of admirable living. Perhaps closest to Moore's intention is the claim that to understand Christian belief and language we must understand the way of life with which they are associated, typically and normatively. That applies to the *teachings* of Jesus, which enjoin a certain way of life, but it is less plausible for *doctrines* about Jesus, such as his divinity, his resurrection, and his place in the Trinity, where the implications for human life are not so obvious.

Near the end of his book, Moore gestures toward a less reductionist account of divine action. He suggests that an event such as a lucky rescue from danger or death, an unpredictable coincidence of independent factors, can be ascribed to God, not as a supernatural agent, but rather because the believer sees the event not as *mere* coincidence but as having significance (234). But the relevant significance is more than just an ordinary human reaction of "Phew, that was a lucky escape, I could have died." It goes beyond our beliefs about "the natural scheme of things . . . to introduce a disturbance into our language and into our lives" (257), to express wonder at what has happened (259, 268), to be impressed (262), to find special significance (263–4). Seeing such significance in events "is not an arbitrary thing, it depends on the wider context of a person's life" (265), it is a recognition of how things "*should* be looked at, not taken for granted" (269). An event that is a genuine coincidence according to our knowledge of the workings of the world can said to be "*in a deeper sense,* not really a coincidence at all"; we thus "express a *deeper insight* into what it is" (232–3; the author's italics). But could this be applied not only to fortunate coincidences (which invite description as miracles) but also to unfortunate events, e.g., when a slate falls on someone's head or a child contracts a deadly disease. Can *those* be equally seen as significant, as God's action or God's will? Is that the deeper insight that is relevant? Moore appends an important parenthetical remark here:

> So in religion generally, if we say that things are not what they appear to be, it is not that they are something else, so that appearances are deceitful; it is that you need insight, a deeper understanding—of things as they appear to be—to see them as they really are. Here is a glimpse of the function of the words "real,""really" in a religious context. When we say, "God really exists" or, "God is what is ultimately real," etc., what is going on in those sentences is not likely to be unrelated to my remarks here. (233)

In contrast to the non-realist and relativist tenor of some Moore's Wittgensteinian analysis, there seems to be some assumption here about how things really are, together with an epistemological claim that we (at least some of us, in the right conditions) can attain insight into how things are. But what exactly is the ontological claim here?—It remains somewhat obscure. Moore says "God" is not the name of an agent but also "God is an agent, for he does things" (235). That seems contradictory, but the point is presumably the old but evasive claim that God's agency is quite different from human agency (236).

Moore goes on to affirm that "God is not to be understood by trying to strain beyond what can be seen, by 'transcending the world of the senses,' but by *resisting* the temptation to do that, by learning to be happy with what we have" (237). That threatens to reduce belief in God to being content with our lot in life. On the next page he says dramatically "there is nothing that *counts* as understanding God; *there is nothing to be understood*" (238; the author's italics). But that seems to deny the ontology and epistemology implicit in the above-quoted passage and to contradict the claim that God-talk expresses a deeper insight into how things are. In this intriguing book Moore often appears to be sitting on the fence, facing both ways, which is hardly a comfortable position! But I will appropriate some of his Wittgensteinian insights about the context of religious belief in a form of life in Part III.

PART III

EXPERIENCES

Parts I and II were predominantly intellectual, reviewing some of the most influential concepts and theories of God, and various non-realist interpretations of theological language. Part III tries to get nearer to living religion by examining some accounts of religious faith and experience of the divine. From that enormous field, I have selected a few that have impressed me in one way or another.

14

RELIGIOUS EXPERIENCE

Various people down the ages have claimed to encounter God directly for themselves: "mysticism" is the general word for it. If an experience is said to be *of God*, the person making such a claim (for themselves, or about someone else) must have some conception of God in mind, however undefined. The experience is understood as different from a memory of a deceased father, a dream of an embrace by an absent lover, or a hallucination caused by a fever, a drug, or an ill-digested dinner. In *those* cases, there will be independently verifiable facts about the dead father, the lover somewhere abroad, or the *non*-existence of pink spiders crawling up the walls. But notoriously there are no such commonly agreed facts about God as the alleged object of religious experience. Religious authorities do not automatically accept every claim to a vision of God, Jesus, Mary, Muhammad, or the Buddha, but they may send round a committee of supposed experts to question the claimant and the circumstances. Their criteria for validation presumably include the theological orthodoxy of the claim. A history of mental illness may tell against it, but what passes for mental health may not be sufficient.

In an influential book first published in 1917 and translated with the title *The Idea of the* Holy,[1] the German theologian Rudolf Otto (1869–1937) traced the development of what he called the *non*-rational element in religion from its anthropological beginnings to what he saw as its highest culmination in Christianity.[2] He argued that in almost all forms of human religion there is a core kind of experience which goes beyond rational apprehension and description, though it need not be *anti*-rational for in "higher" religions it gets interpreted in theological and philosophical categories. Otto opposed one-sided intellectual interpretations according to which the essence of deity can be given in concepts, like those we examined in Part I. Even the most systematic theologians allow a place for religious experience that goes beyond mere rationality,[3] and apophatic theologians naturally agree.

The words "holy" or "sacred" apply to people, places, buildings, statues, icons, relics, rituals, or institutions that are seen by their devotees as having deep religious significance, and in such usage those terms imply very (or absolutely) *good*.[4] But Otto argues that if we strip off this moral element in the concept of the holy, we can discern a more primitive core, for which he coined the term "the numinous," meaning the awareness of something mysterious, impressive, and "awful" in the sense of arousing not just fear but *awe*. This numinous state of mind is irreducible to any other, it cannot be defined or taught, it can only be *evoked* when certain objects or situations stimulate or "awake" our innate capacity for it. Otto boldly claims that the faculty of "divination," i.e., of "cognizing and recognizing the holy in its appearances," is a priori in Kant's sense (161, 192–5). It may not be equally developed in everyone, yet some degree of responsiveness to the numinous seems to be a human universal.

Otto talks of numinous states of mind, while insisting that the numinous is typically felt as objective and outside the self (25). But this does not imply that there *always* exists some appropriate external object, for someone can have a vivid feeling of a ghostly presence in a deserted building at midnight without there being anything there other than dark shapes and shadows, bats and spiders, creaking doors and gusts of wind. In philosophical terminology, the feeling of the numinous always has an internal or "intentional" object, but may or may not have a real external object.

In a lengthy central chapter, Otto distinguishes a number of elements within the feeling of the numinous or "*mysterium tremendum*" as he calls it: awfulness, overpoweringness, energy or urgency, fascination, the uncanny (26–55). But he is concerned to distinguish primitive forms of this from the more developed forms that he applauds in parts of the Hebrew Bible, the New Testament, and in Martin Luther. He mentions the feeling of "dependence," on which Schleiermacher tried to build theology, but Otto insists that there is a specifically *religious* kind of dependence that he calls "creature-consciousness," namely the feeling of being "overwhelmed by one's own nothingness in contrast to that which is supreme above all creatures" (24). He cites *Genesis* 18:27: "May

I make so bold as to speak unto the Lord, who am nothing but dust
and ashes," and *Isaiah* 6:1–8: "Woe is me! I am doomed, for my
own eyes have seen the King, the Lord of Hosts." And at the end of
the book that bears his name, Job declares:

> *I have spoken of things which I have not understood,*
> *things too wonderful for me to know . . . now I see you*
> *with my own eyes. . . . Therefore I yield, repenting in dust*
> *and ashes. (42:1–6)*

Otto says this passage displays the mysterious or numinous in rare
purity and completeness and "may well rank among the most remarkable in the history of religion" (93). He also mentions the
eleventh chapter of the Bhagavad Gita as "one of the perfectly classical passages for the theory of Religion." In the middle of this
long Hindu poem, the Supreme Self or Spirit, or Lord, appears to
Arjuna as infinitely powerful and authoritative but destructive as
well as creative:

> *Vishnu, the great Lord of Yoga,*
> *Revealed his supreme, majestic*
> *form to him, the son of Pritha.*
>
> *That form has many eyes and mouths,*
> *and many wonders visible,*
> *With many sacred ornaments,*
> *And many scared weapons raised. . . .*

You, the unchanging object of all knowledge,
you, the ultimate refuge of this cosmos,
you, the eternal law's immortal champion,
and, as I now believe, primeval spirit! . . .

So terrifying your mouths in appearance,
resembling the fires of destruction,
disoriented, I can find no refuge,
O Lord of Gods, O World-Abode, have mercy![5]

Irreverent comparison to the experience of the numinous could be the first stirrings of sexual attraction in adolescence, or hearing a Beethoven symphony, or the voice of Elvis Presley in his prime. Otto mentions the erotic (61–2) and music as analogies for the numinous (though he lived too early to hear Presley):

> *(Music) releases a blissful rejoicing in us, and we are conscious of a glimmering, billowy agitation occupying our minds, without being able to express or explain in concepts what it really is that moves us so deeply. (63)*

In Kant's *Critique of Judgment* there is a similar claim that aesthetic experience goes beyond our concepts.

> *By an aesthetic idea I mean a presentation of the imagination which prompts much thought, but to which no determinate thought whatsoever, i.e. no determinate*

> *concept, can be adequate, so that no language can express*
> *it completely and allow us to grasp it.*[6]

It is not that we cannot apply *any* concepts, for we may know perfectly well that we are hearing a tenor voice and piano or looking at a mountain landscape or an oil painting. But our concepts do not capture the full nature of our aesthetic experience: we perceive more than we can say.[7] In poetry and drama *words* are used, but their effects often outrun the meanings explicitly deployed.

The numinous is very close to the notion of the sublime, as Otto notes (56, 61, 78). We tend to reserve the term "sublime" for something involving more than ordinary beauty, an extra dimension of depth, mystery, and power. A person, a dress, a flower, a view, a tune, a pussycat, or a wallpaper can be pretty, perhaps even beautiful, but hardly *sublime* compared to Bach's B-minor Mass or St. Matthew Passion, the Cairngorm Mountains, the ocean in a storm, a crocodile,[8] a tiger,[9] the French Revolution,[10] or (more peacefully) the paintings by Palmer and Vermeer mentioned in Chapter 1. Kant's treatment of the sublime is typically difficult and wordy, but in one passage he approaches Otto's notion of the numinous:

> *Thus any spectator who beholds massive mountains*
> *climbing skyward, deep gorges with raging streams in*
> *them, wastelands lying in deep shadow and inviting mel-*
> *ancholy meditation, and so on is indeed seized by amaze-*
> *ment bordering on terror, by horror and a sacred thrill.*[11]

Kant insists that our feeling for the sublime is not fear, for we can be deeply impressed by such scenes when viewing them from a place of safety. In his analysis there is an ambiguity like Otto's, between the outer objects and the mental states they tend to induce in us; Kant's official position is that what is primarily sublime is the peculiar agitating yet uplifting mental effect certain scenes can have on us when they arouse our awareness of our own mental powers, our morality, and our dignity. [12] But it is easy to lapse into describing the objects themselves as sublime.

In our perceptions of beauty and sublimity we transcend the impulses of biology, money, fame, or power. Even with matters that *do* concern our survival and reproduction, many of our experiences involve sensitivity to factors that our words do not fully capture. Our senses of smell and taste have evolved to guide what to eat and what to avoid, but (paltry as our sense of smell is compared with many other animals) we can make discriminations that outrun the words we have learnt. We are sensitive to those tones of voice, facial expressions, and bodily movements that express another person's state of mind, including erotic interactions and the antics of our children. [13] And we can recognize other individuals by their faces without being able to supply a verbal description that would satisfy the police. [14] There is much in common human experience that goes beyond verbal expression.

But this is hardly enough to justify Otto's theory that the capacity for distinctively *religious* experience is an a priori universal in human nature, let alone the claim that the most satisfactory object of numinous experience is God in the Christian conception. Empirically, it looks as if religious feeling is as unevenly distributed among humans as artistic or mathematical talent, though Otto's claim can be qualified as saying that there is a basic capacity for numinous experience which varies, perhaps even genetically (as musical and mathematical ability do), and whose level of development depends on familial and cultural influences.

A deeper problem is that whereas with mathematics and music there are criteria for correct judgment,[15] it is—to put it mildly—far from clear that we have any agreed criteria for truth in religion. Crusading atheists may say that experience of the numinous involves a systematic *illusion* in which we misapply our evolved mental module for interpreting the mental states of other people to cases where there is really no other mind at all, as when we "see" a face in the moon or feel fear of ghosts. Otto himself mentions the feeling of weirdness, the uncanny, the spooky, as a primitive case of the numinous (29, 54). The earliest forms of religion may well depend on such feelings, but it is difficult to be sure about such hypotheses, for we should not read back our own conceptions and feelings ("civilized" as we are supposed to be) into the minds of our distant ancestors.

Otto made a strong case for the existence and the centrality of non-rational numinous elements in religious experience, but when it comes to judgments of value about *which* forms of religious experience count as highest (most "true," in some sense?), he has to appeal to more conceptual and rational factors. In one place he sketches a hierarchy of levels from mere "daemonic dread,"[16] through worship of gods in the plural, to the highest level of all, where the worship of God is "at its purest" (31). We have to acknowledge that experience of the numinous or holy can take questionable forms. Veneration of relics, "weeping" statues, holy texts, or charismatic individuals may be naïve traditional piety, but can extend into superstition and fanaticism. The influence of cults or political movements can overwhelm rationality and morality. Hitler was greeted with adoration as "the Savior of Germany" in the years of his rise to power before World War II and the extermination camps. Some cult leaders have convinced their followers to break with their families or to commit suicide or acts of terrorism. The intensity of feelings is no guarantee of the quality of their objects.

The idiosyncratic Danish religious philosopher Soren Kierkegaard (1815–1855) asserted the supreme importance of individual experience and choice in Christian faith. In a famous passage of a central work he introduced his controversial notion of "subjective truth":

> *When the question of truth is raised in an objective manner, reflection is directed objectively to the truth, as an object to which the knower is related. . . .When the question of the truth is raised subjectively, reflection is directed subjectively to the nature of the individual's relationship: if only the mode of this relationship is in the*

> *truth, the individual is in the truth, even if he should*
> *happen to be related to what is not true. . . .*
>
> *If one who lives in the midst of Christianity goes up*
> *to the house of God, the house of the true God, with the*
> *true conception of God in his knowledge, and prays, but*
> *prays in a false spirit; and one who lives in an idolatrous*
> *community prays with the entire passion of the infinite,*
> *although his eyes rest on an idol: where is there most*
> *truth? The one prays in truth to God though he worships*
> *an idol; the other prays falsely to the true God, and hence*
> *worships in fact an idol. . . .*
>
> *The objective accent falls on WHAT is said, the subjec-*
> *tive accent falls on HOW it is said.*[17]

But there is a similar danger here. People can notoriously fall in love with very unsuitable persons. They can get passionately involved in political parties or campaigns, in religious fanaticism or cults, or in serial child abuse. Even harmless but strongly held commitments—such as collecting the stamps of Ruritania, building model military fortifications in one's garden,[18] or climbing all the Munros[19]—are no guarantee of the worth of their objects. In the intensity of his reaction against Hegelian philosophizing (which he repeatedly repudiates as mere "speculation," devoid of genuine individual commitment), Kierkegaard seems to lapse into an encomium of subjectivity that might permit eccentricity, idolatry, or worse. I will discuss whether there is a more defensible interpretation of his notion of religious faith in Chapter 16.

As we will see, also in Chapter 16, Kant offered an interpretation of religion that privileges rationality and morality but tends to deny or underplay religious experience, whereas Otto's account of the lower level of the numinous (with "the moral element stripped off") does the reverse. Kant admitted a certain kind of awe, however, in a much-quoted sentence at the end of his second *Critique*:

> *Two things fill the mind with ever new and increasing admiration and reverence (Ehrfurcht), the more often and more steadily one reflects on them: the starry heavens above me and the moral law within me.*[20]

Otto emphasizes the process of rationalization and moralization by which the numinous attracts and appropriates "meanings derived from the social and individual ideals of obligation, justice, and goodness," with the final outcome in which the holy becomes both good and sacrosanct, a process that "we prize as the ever-growing self-revelation of the divine" (127–8). In that last phrase there is some sort of claim to realism and truth.

15

THE ETERNAL THOU

The Jewish philosopher of religion Martin Buber (1878–1965) is most famous for his short book *I and Thou*.[1] Aphoristic and poetic rather than philosophically or theologically systematic, and written (he said later) in the "inward necessity of a vision," it has been very influential on religious thought. The Postscript added toward the end of his life provides some helpful clarifications.

Buber's basic theme is the distinction between two kinds of relations, and he seems more concerned with the nature of the *relationships* than the conceptualization of their objects. As a first approximation, he distinguishes the I-Thou relation to other people from the I-It relation typical of our dealings with inanimate things. When he portentously declares that the Thou relation "is the cradle of the Real Life" (24), and that "all real living is meeting" (26), we might be tempted to assume that I-Thou relationships are good, whereas I-It relations are not—but that is apparently *not* his intention. He suggests pessimistically that the development of so many new uses of things "comes about mostly through the decrease of man's power to enter into relation" (48), but he would surely have to agree that there is nothing intrinsically wrong with placing a stone to hold down a tent, turning on a washing machine, or using a computer. Conversely, many I-Thou relationships are far from ideal: resentment, rivalry, jealousy, or hatred are attitudes one can form only to a person. Admittedly one can have an *almost* I-It relation to an employee, a customer, or a servant, though even there is some minimal degree of communication. In extremity one could use someone's weight to stabilize a tent if they were unconscious, which would be an I-It relation to a human body.

It may come as a surprise that Buber holds that an I-Thou relation (or something like it) can apply to animals and even to a tree. He remarks that with tame animals we sometimes "win from them an astonishing active response . . . which is stronger . . . in proportion as our attitude is a genuine saying of *Thou*" (117). This is obvious with dogs, though less so with cats, and it can apply between zoo animals and their keepers. Dogs can understand a variety of words, and they respond with communicative sounds or behaviors (as do chimpanzees raised by humans). Buber remarks that an animal's eyes "have the power to speak a great language" (94)—in a metaphorical sense, obviously. With some animals he says we experience "the threshold of mutuality" (though presumably not with worms or spiders).

Plants cannot respond to us, but Buber suggests mysteriously that even with them "there is a reciprocity of the being itself, a reciprocity which is nothing but being in its course" (117). He

cites the reverential attitude one can adopt to a beautiful or ancient tree, which is quite different from the scientific curiosity
of the ecologist, the safety concern of the town planner, or the
commercial interest of the timber-merchant. In Buber's flowery
phraseology, one can "vouchsafe to the tree its unity and wholeness," "become bound up in relation to it," and "seized by the
power of its exclusiveness" (23). It is harder to envisage this applied to a weed or a blade of grass, unless perhaps one is struck
by its beauty under the microscope. Buber insists "we have to do
justice, in complete candor, to the reality which discloses itself to
us"; and he describes the "large sphere, stretching from stones to
stars, as that of the pre-threshold or preliminal" (118). Even inanimate objects like the Rocky Mountains, the Great Barrier Reef,
and Kant's starry heavens can be objects of the I-Thou relation
or something akin to it, like the experience of the sublime we
touched on in the last chapter.

Buber was especially concerned to apply the I-Thou relation to God. But let us first take note, as he does, of a different
part of "the sphere above the threshold, the superliminal" (118),
namely our relation to works of art. The artist, poet, or composer
"is faced by a form which desires to be made through him into a
work," he does not create purely "out of his own soul" but feels the
pressure of something beyond himself which is demanding to be
produced, to be "led across into the world of *It*" (24–5). Buber's
talk of "form" suggests the theory of Forms, and he could recruit
Plato's classic account in the *Symposium* of the soul's ascent from
particular, beautiful things to the vision of the Form of Beauty

itself. But he suggests a mysterious kind of *mutuality* that does not hold with Platonic Forms, and he speaks of "meetings with the Spirit which blows around us and in us" (120):

> *[C]ertain events in man's life, which can scarcely be described, which experience spirit as meeting; and in the end, when indirect indication is not enough, there is nothing for me but to appeal, my reader, to the witness of your own mysteries—buried, perhaps, but still attainable. (118)*

This striking passage comes in the context of a discussion of artistic creation, but Buber's point applies to all of us insofar as we experience ideas, emotions, memories, or impulses just "coming" to us involuntarily.[2] Not all ideas "demand" to be embodied in an artistic work (some may be better suppressed), but they have a life of their own, they can impose on us a kind of *obligation* to judge, or feel, or act in a certain way.

Once an artistic work has been embodied in physical form other people can relate to it. There can be I-It relations to an artwork, as when a painting is hung to impress one's guests or an erotic novel or pop-song generates profits. But when one gets to know the great work of someone long dead, like Shakespeare or Rembrandt or Beethoven, there is a sense in which one comes to "hear his voice," one "receives only the indivisible wholeness of something spoken." In some cases the identity of the creator is lost in history (like Homer), yet one can be deeply impressed by the spirit expressed in an anonymous poem, an ancient Doric pillar, or a traditional folk song (119).

I have spent some time examining the nonreligious applications of Buber's thought, because his project (like Otto's) was to locate our relationship to God in the context of an anthropology, an understanding of human nature and capacities, a theme he explored further in subsequent books. He twice declares in *I and Thou* (21–2, 98) that there are *three* levels of relationships—with nature, with people, and with "spiritual beings." In the latter:

> *the relation is clouded, yet it discloses itself; it does not use speech, yet begets it. We perceive no* Thou, *but none the less we feel we are addressed and we answer—forming, thinking, acting. We speak the primary word with our being, though we cannot utter* Thou *with our lips. (22)*

Buber opens his more theological Part III with the pronouncement that "the extended lines of relations meet in the eternal *Thou*" and "every particular *Thou* is a glimpse through to the eternal *Thou*" (77, 92, 106, 123). He also writes of the living Centre (53–4, 97, 108–9), the Face (58, 60), the primal Source (97), and the absolute Person (125), where the capitalizations presumably indicate that these are alternative descriptions of God.

An atheist reader may be unimpressed by this onslaught of capital letters and may reply "Oh yeah, I've heard that sort of flabby argument before, it tends to go like this":

You love your husband, don't you?
—Well, yes (Some of the time, anyway).
So, you don't treat him as a thing, but as a person?
—Sure (though we have our moments).
Well, there you go: not everything can be explained scientifically,
    there is personality in the universe, therefore God exists!
—Of course there's personality in human persons, *but that doesn't*
    prove there is personality anywhere else.

We may reasonably ask whether Buber can do better than that. But we need to remind ourselves that he is not engaging in the tedious intellectual sport of trying to construct a philosophical argument for God's existence. Rather he is calling attention to some fundamental features of human life, hoping to identify not just consciously "religious" experiences but features of our lives for which talk of God makes sense, albeit perhaps a paradoxical sort of sense.

Buber's emphasis on the I-Thou relation leads him toward his claim that "God is the Being that is directly, most nearly, and lastingly, over against us, that may properly only be addressed, not expressed" (81). That suggests that we cannot "properly" say anything *about* God, we can only say things *to* him. But the quoted sentence itself takes the linguistic form of a statement about God, so it seems Buber has difficulty in following his own precept. A few pages earlier he says: "all God's names are hallowed, for in them he is not merely spoken about, but also spoken to" (77), where the "not merely" suggests that we *can* legitimately speak *about* God in some contexts. In this perplexing book Buber does say, or at least suggests, quite a bit about God, so it would be an interesting exercise to see if it can be recast either into second-*person* addresses to God (prayers) or into *second-order* (theological) statements about human addresses to God.[3] As we have seen, many other thinkers admit that we put language under strain whenever we try to speak of God.

In one passage Buber claims that even someone who has no use for the G-*word* can nevertheless be addressing God:

> *He who speaks the word God and really has* Thou *in mind (whatever the illusion by which he is held), addresses the true* Thou *of his life . . .*
>
> *But when he, too, who abhors the name, and believes himself to be godless, give his whole being to addressing the* Thou *of his life, as a* Thou *that cannot be limited by another, he addresses God. (77–8)*

To this our local atheist may again protest that she is being recruited into theism by verbal sleight of hand. She may turn up her nose at this talk of "addressing the true Thou of her life," but even if she tolerates it as poetic description of situations in which she has to make decisions involving the values that she recognizes, she will not accept that it amounts to addressing *God*. The concept of God has been bequeathed to us freighted with biblical associations of supernatural revelations and punishments, and theological notions of omnipotence and omniscience (and masculinity), and many of us feel queasy about all that. Buber acknowledges that many people reject the word "God" because it has been so misused, and that it is "the most heavily laden of all the words used by men"— yet despite that he maintains it is indispensable. But to justify that he needs to explain what the ethical and existentially minded atheist is missing.

In his Postscript, Buber poses a version of that question, when he asks whether the notion of a response or address coming from outside everything to which we normally attribute consciousness has "any other validity than that of a personifying metaphor" (120). Previously he had affirmed that "the relation with man is the real simile of the relation with God; in it true address receives true response; except that in God's response everything, the universe, is made manifest in language" (99). That means that relationship to God, though in *some* ways similar to human relations, is very different. In the final section of his Postscript, Buber says we can only speak of God in his personal relationship to us, and even that is paradoxical.

> The description of God as a Person is indispensable for everyone . . . who means by "God" . . . him who . . . enters into a direct relation with us men in creative, revealing, and redemptive acts. . . . The concept of personal being is indeed completely incapable of declaring what God's

> *essential being is, but it is both permitted and necessary*
> *to say that God is also a Person. (124)*

Our atheist (if she has stayed with this discussion) might say, "Well, I can see that this talk is quite subtle, with its similes, metaphors, and paradoxes, but I just don't feel any compulsion to play this language-game." That is a familiar stand-off. Perhaps Buber would agree that he can take the atheist horse to spiritual water but can't make her drink, since there is an irreducible element of human choice. But I suspect he would not give up, for he hoped to persuade everyone to recognize that there is a religious dimension to all human life. To that end he offers an interesting non-standard account of revelation (104–6) as a moment in which "a man does not pass, from the moment of supreme meeting, the same being as he entered into it." The word "supreme" suggests that meeting *with God* is meant, but on the human level there can be "supreme" or highly significant meetings in which, for example, I might quite suddenly realize that I love someone, or a word or a gesture reveals that she no longer loves me.

Buber's account of artistic creation suggests that in a metaphorical sense the artist can be said to "meet" an idea for a new work coming "out of the blue," an idea that might dominate her life for years to come. But our atheist may resist Buber's idea that we receive "not a specific content but a Presence, a Presence as power." (Those Blessed Capital Letters again, she will say, trying to smuggle God in by the back door.) She may prefer to go with Nietzsche (whose style, if not his content, seems to have influenced Buber) and say that there is no reason to think that is *anyone there* who "gives," apart from human givers of course. Religious believers personify freely, and they may say that God gives us life and guides us in life. Yet Buber seems to imply that that is an *optional* poetic gloss on human experiences.

There is one more passage that is relevant here where Buber says grandly that "man's religious situation, his being *there in* the Presence, is characterized by its essential and indissoluble antinomy" (93). He is slow to explain what the antinomy consists in, but comes up with:

> [I]f I know that "I am given over for disposal" and know at the same time that "It depends on myself," then I cannot try to escape the paradox . . . I am compelled to take both to myself, to be lived together, and in being lived they are one. (93–4)

There is a general truth here which is not peculiar to religious experience. Although some directions of our attention are under our own control, and we sometimes make consciously deliberated decisions, much of what passes through our minds happens involuntarily, as Freud, Proust, and much literature have shown. But when made explicit there is little surprise here, not even an *apparent* contradiction between two propositions as in Kant's famous antinomies. To be sure, there are practical decisions to be made in the light of experiences and ideas which we perhaps have not chosen: life has to be *lived*. Believers will apply this to their relations to God and say that his revelation and grace are beyond our control, yet are of supreme significance to our lives. Buber makes it understandable how some people can interpret their lives in terms of an I-Thou relation to "the eternal *Thou*"; perhaps he would agree that is all he can hope to do.[4]

16

MORAL FAITH

Immanuel Kant's reputation as a thoroughly rational and deeply difficult philosopher may lead many readers to assume that he is one of the very last persons to whom to look for anything positive about religion and faith. Yet he declared that he was denying knowledge to make room for faith. His views on religion (primarily Christianity) evolved through his long life (1724–1804), but I will concentrate on his mature "critical" thought. (Those who feel allergic to heavyweight Kantian philosophy could skip this chapter, but they would be passing up an opportunity to learn a bit about Kant, without tears.[1])

Kant was arguably the deepest thinker of the Enlightenment, that movement of thought centered in eighteenth-century Europe, and extending to the youthful United States of America, that sought to apply reason to all human affairs. That makes him suspect to those theologians who remain deeply suspicious of the Enlightenment's appeal to human reason. Late in his life, when his international reputation was well-established, Kant's writing on religion incurred the disapproval of Prussian censorship under Friedrich Wilhelm II, who forbade him to publish any more on the topic.[2] On the other hand, his qualified defense of religious faith attracted the scorn of Goethe (a very different figure in the German Enlightenment) who remarked sardonically that Kant had "slobbered on his philosopher's cloak" by allowing Christianity into his philosophy by the back door. Kant was indeed somewhat ambiguous about religion. He was brought up in the Pietist tradition, a radical branch of Lutheranism that emphasized religious feeling and virtuous living as more important than creedal orthodoxy and ecclesiastical ritual, and that ethos stayed with him throughout his life. But there was also a strong influence from physical science and from the highly rationalist style of German philosophy in which he had been educated.

In his "pre-critical" phase before arriving at his world-famous "critical philosophy," Kant defended a strongly metaphysical conception of God as the real ground of all possibilities, arguing (like the classic medieval theologians considered in Chapter 3) that God is a necessary being; unique, simple, immutable and eternal; containing supreme reality; yet in some sense a mind.[3] He devoted a 100-page book to this theme, which he obviously took very seriously at that stage of his thought. Yet at the end of that intricately argued work, he admitted that it is "more important . . . to inspire man with noble feelings, which are richly productive of noble actions, than to instruct him with carefully weighed syllogisms"; and in the very last sentence, he declared that though it is necessary for a people to *believe* that God exists, it is not so necessary to prove it.[4] It seemed that Kant's Pietism was already outweighing his rationalism. That was confirmed in another pre-critical work where he asked: "Does not the heart of man contain within itself immediate moral prescriptions? Is it really necessary, in order to induce man to act in accordance with his destiny here on earth, to set the machinery moving in another world?"[5]

In the Dialectic section of the ground-breaking difficult masterpiece that forms the foundation of the "critical" philosophy, the *Critique of Pure Reason* of 1781, Kant rejected all three traditional proofs of the existence of God: the ontological argument (from the mere concept of God), the cosmological argument (that a necessary being must explain the contingent world—as we noted in Chapter 3), and the "physico-theological" argument (for a divine designer of the world—see Chapter 7).[6] That epoch-making first *Critique* developed an elaborate theory of the extent and limits of human knowledge. Our cognition of the material world must be based on "intuition" (*Anschauung*), i.e., sense-perception, organized by our fundamental a priori concepts ("the categories"), and our factual knowledge cannot extend to anything beyond those bounds. So the time-honored metaphysical propositions about the existence of God, the immortality of the soul, and the freedom of our will cannot be known, whether by purely philosophical argument or by the methods of empirical science. But it was important to Kant that they cannot be *dis*proved either.

So these three propositions remained meaningful hypotheses or "postulates,"[7] and Kant argued that we need to believe in them, but only from the practical, and above all *moral*, point of view. When we are deciding what we should aim for and what to do, rather than what to believe, a different sort of reasons become relevant: reasons for action, whether self-interested or moral. Kant saw an essential connection between religious belief and ethics, rather than with supposed metaphysical knowledge. Hence that famous line in which he declared that he "had to deny *knowledge* (*Wissen*) in order to make room for *faith* (*Glaube*)."[8] Near the end of the first *Critique*, he gave a first indication of his distinctively *moral* arguments for God and immortality[9]:

> [N]o one will be able to boast that he knows *that there is a God and a future life*. . . . No, the conviction in them is not logical but moral, and since it depends on subjective grounds (of moral disposition) I must not even say "It is *morally* certain that there is a God,"but rather "I am *morally* certain."[10]

This passage strikes a surprisingly existentialist note, anticipating the subjective emphasis of Kierkegaard in the next century. Kant here recognized a deep difference between religious faith on the hand and theoretical beliefs, opinions, and hypotheses on the other: faith is distinctively personal and individual, involving one's attitude to the whole of one's life.[11] Accordingly, he distinguished three kinds of propositional attitude: "having an opinion" (*meinen*) is taking something to be true while being aware that one's evidence for it is *in*sufficient; "knowing" (*wissen*) is taking something to be true with *sufficient* evidence for it; but Kant defines "believing" or "having faith" (both English terms have been used to translate the German verb *glauben*) is taking something as "subjectively sufficient" while being aware that evidence is *in*sufficient.[12] Kierkegaard hit on a similar formulation in his definition of subjective truth, which he said is "an equivalent expression for faith":

> *An objective uncertainty held fast in an appropriation-process of the most passionate inwardness is the truth, the highest truth available for an existing individual.*[13]

Kant developed his "moral theology" in detail in his second and third *Critiques*.[14] This is not the place to go into the continuing philosophical debates about just how to interpret his austerely rational conception of moral obligation, but it is worth noting that he claimed at one point that it coincides in application with Jesus's summary of the commandments: to love God and to love one's neighbor as oneself.[15] Kant argued that our motivation for moral action would be undermined unless we have faith in divine providence and justice. We can know what our moral duties *are* without appeal to God's reported commandments, and we should fulfill them without any promise of divine reward, even in an afterlife, but we still need some sort of general hope that doing the right thing will tend to enhance human well-being in the long term.[16]

There, perhaps, is a topic for "moral faith" that does not explicitly involve belief in God or immortality.

In Kant's formulation we have a duty to promote "the highest good," the ultimate combination of happiness in proportion to virtue; so the highest good must be *possible*, for "ought" implies "can": there can be no obligation to achieve what is impossible for us. In the second, practical *Critique*, Kant assumed that only an omniscient, omnipotent, and beneficent God can bring about the highest good, the coincidence of virtue and happiness, and this can only be in a life after death, since it is painfully obvious that virtue is not always rewarded with happiness in life as we know it.[17] However there is an ambiguity in the claim that we have a duty to act for the highest good: it is plausible only if it means *not* actually and fully to *achieve* it (which is beyond any of us, at any stage of history), but rather to do whatever we can to *help* human society *approximate* to the highest good. The latter does not assume that fully achieving it is possible, only that it is an ideal to be constantly held before us as what we must aim for. In that case, divine providence is needed only to guarantee the possibility of some *progress* toward the highest good.

In his formidable late work *Religion within the Bounds of Bare Reason* there were significant new developments in Kant's religious thought.[18] In the first Part, he diagnoses a radical evil in human nature—contrary to the more naïve optimism of many other Enlightenment thinkers. He acknowledges our frailty—our difficulty in doing what we know we ought to do, and our impurity— our tendency to confuse or adulterate moral reasons with other motives. What he sees as radically evil is not our natural desires, but rather the depravity of the human heart, the freely chosen *subordination* of duty to inclination, the preference for one's own happiness (as one conceives of it) over duties to others. The Christian Pietist influence shows up when Kant holds out hope for a return to the good from which we have strayed, for in the second Part of the *Religion* he gives a somewhat convoluted account of the battle of "the good principle" (rather ambiguously personified as "Son of God") for dominion over us. By a change of heart, a revolution in our fundamental disposition, we can become, in a moral and religious sense, a new person.[19]

There emerges a crucial antinomy that has long been problematic in theology, between what God does for us and what we need to do for ourselves.[20] Kant was a firm believer in free will, so he emphasized the latter, but he recognized that we need to believe in a God of forgiveness and grace who in a mysterious way supplements our own efforts to improve ourselves.[21] It is vital that we each hope to be a better person, and that we can all hope for a better world. Despite the discouragements that life throws at us, including our own failures, we must not become complacent or cynical, degenerate or despairing. Kant admitted that we need to *hope* that what does not lie in our power will be "made good by co-operation from above." We come up against the limits of our knowledge, where we can only have hope and faith:

> *[I]t is impossible to make these effects* theoretically
> *cognizable (that they are effects of grace and not of*

> *immanent nature*) . . . *moreover, the* practical employ-
> *ment of this idea is wholly self-contradictory, for . . . to*
> *expect an effect of grace means . . . that the good . . . is*
> *not of our doing.*
>
> *. . . Hence we can admit an effect of grace as some-*
> *thing incomprehensible but cannot incorporate it into*
> *our maxims for either theoretical or practical use.*[22]

Despite this qualified appeal to divine grace, there are passages in the *Religion* where Kant questioned the need to have any definite faith in the *existence* of God. In one of his supersized footnotes he wrote:

> [S]o far as theoretical cognition and profession of faith
> are concerned, no assertoric knowledge is required in
> religion (even of the existence of God) . . . this faith
> needs only the idea of God . . . *without pretending to*
> *secure objective reality for it through theoretical cogni-*
> *tion. Subjectively, the* minimum *of cognition (it is pos-*
> *sible that there is a God) must alone suffice for what can*
> *be made the duty of every human being.*[23]

In this late work Kant's tendency was to interpret the claims of revealed, historical faiths as symbolic of general truths about the human condition, i.e., as "natural" religion "within the limits of reason."[24] He declared that the various religious traditions (including non-Christian religions) should be treated with reverence, as the vessels which have so far carried people's ethics and spirituality, but he hoped that with the progress of education and enlightenment what is inessential in them (in his view) can be transcended, and what is essential strengthened.[25] In Parts three and four of the *Religion*, he envisaged a purified form of churches as "ethical communities," uniting their members as a people of God under moral laws.[26] In all this he influenced nineteenth-century liberal Protestant theology, for better or for worse.[27]

Kant repeatedly declared that religion consists in viewing one's duties *as* God's commands.[28] I think he meant that although we do not need to appeal to any particular commandments allegedly issued by God to know what our duties are, we need some sort of religious or quasi-religious faith in divine grace and providence to find the motivation and inspiration to live up to them. That is a problem that affects us all.[29]

FORGIVENESS AND GRACE

For all his talk of addressing God and being addressed by him, Buber did not offer any examples of what might actually be *said* on either side;[1] and he hardly touches on the central topics of God's love, forgiveness, and grace. He could have pointed to examples from the Hebrew scriptures—but however hallowed by tradition, those are ancient stories about people long dead—sometimes telling of God appearing in physical form, being represented by an angel, or speaking audibly. They are not contemporary first-hand experiences of *I-Thou* relations to God, on which Buber was so keen. The gospels recount stories of encounters with Jesus, but those were with a *human* person (whatever theological interpretation was subsequently made of him). Christians may say that in hearing or reading the gospel stories two millennia later we encounter God for ourselves. Some believers may say they have experienced God "speaking" directly to them (though not usually audibly). Buber's *I and Thou*, for all its fervor and poetry, is philosophy of religion rather than religion itself.

For something closer to real-life religious experience, we can look to more practical devotional writings, of which there are many and various. I will take as one example some impressive passages in a short book by André Louf, abbot of a Cistercian monastery in France. Louf puts repentance—contrition for one's sins, including misdeeds, mis-speakings, serious omissions, and bad thoughts—at the center of the spiritual quest:

> No one can get to know his or her sin without at the same time getting to know God—not before or afterwards, but simultaneously in one and the same moment of spiritual insight.
>
> Anyone who thinks he knows his sin apart from the encounter with God still lives in a state of illusion. He confuses repentance with a more or less developed feeling of guilt that lies within the experience of every normal human being. . . .
>
> At the very moment that the sinner receives forgiveness and is caught up by God and restored in grace, at that moment—wonder of wonders!—sin has become the place where God enters into contact with a human being. One may even go further and say that there is no other way to encounter God and to learn to know him than by the way of repentance.
>
> . . . Thus God makes himself known by forgiving.[2]

On this account, repentance for one's sin is not just a sufficient but also a *necessary* condition for knowing God. Some may find this a bit extreme: can't one know God in the beauties of nature and art, in spiritual music, or in the beauty of soul that some rare people exhibit? Perhaps Louf would agree but would say that the only real *depth* of encounter with God is in experience that touches one to the core and involves a change of one's own life and that repentance is at the center of any such experience. This fits with Kierkegaard's Christian existentialism.

Let us confront a sample atheist with these thoughts. Unless he is particularly self-satisfied and overconfident, he may admit that he has sometimes failed to do what he should have done and has done some things he shouldn't have done (even if nothing more outrageous than using his sharp tongue on his nearest and dearest). He may admit he occasionally feels guilty, but he will resist theological interpretation of his human failings. He may have given an occasional apology, but in general his attitude might be: "Don't cry over spilt milk, don't obsess about it, just learn from it and get over it, life must go on." Our abbot will surely agree that this degree of regret, apology, and fresh resolve expressed in humanist terms is much better than the state of a person who hurts others and never realizes he has done anything wrong. But Louf obviously believes that it lacks the spiritual depth of true repentance and experience of divine forgiveness.

Where then is the distinction between "true" repentance and common human acknowledgement of guilt? I suggest it lies in the difference between "I have sinned" and "I am a sinner"—or if you don't like the religious word "sin," between "I have done something wrong" and "There is something wrong with me." The former is an acknowledgment of some *specific* action or omission (for which apology or restitution would be appropriate, if possible); the latter is a realization that one has bad *dispositions* or tendencies, which one cannot simply change at will, indeed it is often unclear what one can do about them. One may *resolve* to do better, of course, but resolutions and promises to change behavior are notoriously unreliable. One might go to a psychotherapist, take a course of mindfulness, or try a regimen of cold showers, but the results are not within one's control and are not predictable.

Jesus's parable of the Pharisee and the tax-collector (*Luke* 18:9–14) has the former praying, "I thank you, God, that I am not like the rest of mankind—greedy, dishonest, adulterous—or, for that matter, like this tax-collector here," whereas the latter (reviled as a self-serving collaborator with the Roman occupation) beat his breast and prayed, "God have mercy on me, sinner that I am." Jesus concluded that it was the tax-collector who went home acquitted of his sins. The take-home message is that a necessary condition of forgiveness is that one must acknowledge that one has sinful dispositions and that one needs help to change. Moreover, Jesus's closing words suggest that divine acquittal follows immediately on sincere repentance, perhaps even that repentance is a sufficient condition of forgiveness. We might worry that it makes it too easy if all one had to do is to acknowledge that one is a sinner, and then all guilt is automatically wiped away.[3] We can hardly approve of the person who goes regularly to confession and receives absolution but who feels little compunction about repeating her sins because she is assured that forgiveness is always available. Paul asked: "Shall we persist in sin, so that there may be all the more grace?" and answered: "Certainly not! We died to sin, how can we live in it any longer?" (*Romans* 6:1–2).

The answer to this worry must lie in a more demanding conception of repentance. It is not enough to utter a form of words (which may not be seriously meant), and it is not enough to experience guilt-feelings (which may not go very deep, and may get overlaid with other feelings and distractions). The demand is for "a change of heart." But what does that familiar phrase mean?—it is a metaphor, after all (no cardiac arrest or change of blood-flow need be involved). *Metanoia* in the New Testament is not just any change of mind or re-evaluation of values, it is more even than the change of "fundamental project" that Sartre mentions as a rare possibility at the end of his monumental work of existential ontology *Being and Nothingness*. It requires, firstly, an acknowledgment of the rules one has broken and of the ideals one has failed to live up to; secondly, an acknowledgment that one finds it difficult to change (one's pride is punctured, one realizes that one needs help); and thirdly, that one should not stay in a state of despair, self-hatred, or self-harm (still obsessed with *oneself*). One needs to realize that help toward change is possible, start to seek it, and get on with the job of restoring relationships with other people.

The reader will notice that I am roaming around the borderlands between theological and secular analyses: Perhaps that is a good place to roam these days?[4] Our atheist might be

brought to something resembling the above change of heart by a
sudden outburst from a long-suffering spouse or employee (when
the worm turns!), by a remark from a candid friend, or possibly
when watching a relevant scene in a film or play (remember the
effect of the play within the play on the guilty king in *Hamlet*). If
suitably chastened, the atheist might accept the description I gave
at the end of the previous paragraph but may stubbornly ask why
the G-word has to come into it.

At this point it may be useful to turn to someone who offered
a different vocabulary for these subtle spiritual matters, namely
the German-born American theologian Paul Tillich (1886–1965),
who hoped to explain the Christian faith by "correlating" it to
questions that arise for everyone, believers and nonbelievers alike.
In a famous sermon entitled "You are accepted" he said:

> *We do not have a knowledge of sin unless we have already*
> *experienced the unity of life, which is grace. And con-*
> *versely, we could not grasp the meaning of grace without*
> *having experienced the separation of life, which is sin.*
>
> *. . . Thus, the state of our whole life is estrangement*
> *from others and ourselves, because we are estranged from*
> *the Ground of our being, because we are estranged from*
> *the origin and aim our life.*
>
> *. . . Grace strikes us when we are in great pain and*
> *restlessness . . . it strikes us when we feel that our sep-*
> *aration is deeper than usual, because we have violated*
> *another life, a life which we have loved, or from which*

we were estranged. . . . Sometimes at that moment a wave
of light breaks into our darkness, and it is as though a
voice were saying: "You are accepted. You are accepted,
accepted by that which is greater than you, and the name
of which you do not know. . . . *Do not seek for anything;*
do not perform anything; perhaps later you will do much;
do not intend anything. Simply accept the fact that
you are accepted!*"If that happens to us, we experience*
grace. . . . In that moment, grace conquers sin, and rec-
onciliation bridges the gulf of estrangement.[5]

This is Tillich's twentieth-century take on Luther's classic doctrine
of justification by faith, itself powerfully based on Paul's epistle
to the Romans. I am circling around this classic Christian theme,
but some readers may be relieved (though others may be disap-
pointed) to know I am not going to discuss the doctrines of in-
carnation and atonement, about which vast quantities of ink (and
I fear, a certain amount of blood) have been spilled.[6]

If we persist rather doggedly with the question whether any
conception of God has to come into it, we can hardly help noticing
that Tillich's account of sin, repentance, and grace (as represented
in this sermon), though mostly couched in psychological terms,
has vestiges or overtones of theology. The crucial idea is being
accepted, but the obvious question is: Accepted *by whom*? Tillich
replies: "that which is greater than you, of which you do not know
the name." It seems God is thereby invoked, but in a very shy (or
sly?) sort of way. In Tillich's interpretation of sin, we are said to

be estranged from "the Ground of our being"—and there goes a Capital Letter again, so no prizes for guessing Who is meant!

Tillich's theological system was strongly influenced by existentialist philosophy, especially Heidegger, who was himself influenced by the medieval German mystic Meister Eckhardt. Tillich developed an austere philosophical conception of God as "the Ground of being," but the very abstract language he used needs a good deal of interpreting, to put it mildly. In his ponderous *Systematic Theology* he wrote, apophatically and provocatively: "God does not exist. He is being-itself beyond essence and existence. Therefore, to argue that God exists is to deny him." He added: "God is being-itself, not *a* being."[7] We may well wonder what is meant by "being-itself": perhaps the idea was to define the G-word in such a way as to make it unquestionable that it denotes something real, so that the only question would be about what *sort* of reality that is.

In that sermon Tillich says it is *as though* a voice speaks to us in our darkness, yet he surely does not mean that this is a mere figment of our imagination but rather that the "voice," though not physically embodied in sound waves, expresses some fundamental *truth*. It is not enough to *fantasize* about being accepted, or half-persuade ourselves of it, we must be convinced that the acceptance is in some sense real, that it goes beyond our own mental states. We can compare this to the child-parent relation. Suppose a child has committed some nontrivial misdemeanor and is justifiably reprimanded and made to feel bad—not just unhappy, but guilty. Having communicated the wrongness of the offense (and the mother would be failing in her duty if she does not), she does not withdraw her fundamental love, but at a suitable moment makes it clear that she still loves her child, and normal relations are restored (until the next time). In Tillich's terms, acceptance persists throughout such an episode, but it needs to be explicitly offered and accepted for the situation to be resolved. In Louf's more traditional terms (which apply to us all, at any age), God's love and forgiveness is always there, but we repeatedly need to realize it and accept it.

Freud and the Freudians may say that this is wish-fulfillment, the projection of the idealized child-parent relation onto the illusory figure of God, the great daddy or mummy in the sky. But theologians can reply conversely that the child-parent relation is a *model* of the real relation between sinful human beings and God. When Tillich proposed that God should be understood as "the Ground of being," he said that is the only literal statement we can make about God and that everything else said about him is symbolic.[8] Yet when we go into this matter of forgiveness and grace, I find myself wanting to say, quite positively, that *God's love is real*, that his forgiveness is always available in response to sincere repentance.[9]

What conception of God is implied by that? Well, at least that we human beings, who have evolved on this planet according to the physical and biological laws of nature, are capable (if rarely) of some degree of unselfish love (*agape* in the New Testament) and mutual forgiveness, and that we can find some mental peace with ourselves, our fellows, and our environment. In other words, the universe is such that this kind of spirituality is *possible*, and moreover it is *necessary* for the best human lives. These are ideals to which we can only approximate, but it is important to have them set before us. This is one interpretation of the saying that we are made in the image of God.[10]

THE INWARD LIGHT

Until recent paragraphs I have been reviewing various conceptions of God in a seemingly uncommitted philosophical manner, but I am well aware that on this subject there can be no such thing as a completely neutral, objective stance. As even such a superbly rational thinker as Immanuel Kant realized, religion involves one's way of life and one's attitude to religious tradition (for or against whichever version one has encountered). I will now outline the approach I have found in the Quaker tradition, as a case study of how conceptions of God need to be taken in life-context and cannot treated as mere intellectual theories.[1] That was a lesson we learnt from Gareth Moore's Wittgensteinian Christianity despite some unclarities in his position. I am not suggesting that Quakerism is the best way, only that it is one good way.

The controversial claim central to the teaching of George Fox and the other early Quakers was that we can perceive divine truth through the "Inward Light."[2] That was not a new idea: many

centuries earlier Augustine gave an account of divine enlightenment in which our minds and words need to be "illuminated" by
God. In words like those that Fox used, Augustine said that we
"need assistance from Christ, the inner teacher, who illuminates
the inner man."[3] But in the troubled times of religious seeking and
civil war in mid-seventeenth-century England, the idea of finding
divine illumination within oneself came as something radically
new. It was liberating to many who joined the growing Quaker
movement. But subversive to those who supported the authority of
the existing churches or the infallibility of the Bible. Here are some
of Fox's most dramatic formulations of his fundamental insight:

> Now the Lord God hath opened to me by his invisible
> power, how that every man was enlightened by the divine
> light of Christ. . . . This I saw in the pure openings of
> the Light, without the help of any man; neither did
> I then know, where to find it in the Scriptures (though
> afterwards, searching the Scriptures, I found it). For I saw
> in that Light and Spirit, which was, before Scripture was
> given forth. . . .
>
> . . . I was commanded to turn people to that inward
> light, spirit and grace, by which all might know their
> salvation, and their way to God; even that divine spirit,
> which would lead them into all Truth, and which I infal-
> libly knew, would never deceive any.[4]

Three centuries later there is a similar passage by Abbot Louf, whom we met in the previous chapter:

> *For a long time, like Saint Augustine, we sought God out-*
> *side ourselves, but in vain. Now we know from experience*
> *that he is within, closer to me than my inmost self. . . .We*
> *will learn to live inwardly, to be* turned inward. *Yet the*
> *moment we have built that bridge to the interior we will*
> *quickly notice that this reality in our inmost being is not*
> *only the core and point of gravity but also the wellspring*
> *from which our whole being will be restructured—the*
> *fountain of power, light and life.*[5]

But is there really available to everyone an "*inward*" Light (with a capital "L") coming from God, that is distinct from the natural light of fallible human reason, socially formed conscience, idiosyncrasy, or fantasy? There is an obvious danger in saying that everyone must follow his or her own inner light, whatever that may show or say. Enlightenment philosophers such as Locke and Kant strongly rejected what they called "enthusiasm," i.e., the claim of competing sects or individuals to have received private revelations from God. Yet in words that echo the prologue to John's gospel, Fox said:

> *the true light which enlightened every man that cometh*
> *into the world was the life in the word and that was*
> *divine and not natural.*[6]

And the Quaker Yearly Meeting in London in 1879 re-affirmed that:

> *The light that shines into man's heart is not of man,*
> *and must ever be distinguished both from the conscience*
> *which it enlightens and from the natural faculty of*
> *reason which, when unsubjected to its holy influences, is,*
> *in the things of God, very foolishness.*[7]

These statements make a sharp distinction between divine and natural light. One might be tempted to picture this as God selectively acting on our minds, sometimes switching the Light on but keeping it off at other times. But one would worry about his reasons for doing so: Surely a loving God would offer his illumination to us all the time? Any obstruction of the divine Light must surely lie on our side.

If we interpret inner illumination merely in terms of judging the truth of propositions, that would be over-intellectual. What about our desires and emotions, our aspirations and ideals: the heart, the spiritual side of us? Surely the function of the divine Light (or Holy Spirit?) is not so much to reveal theological doctrines but to transform our hearts and minds for the better? Isn't it a matter of communicating and awakening love (*agape*—the divine kind of universal unselfish love) rather than information-transfer? Jesus is said to have brought us *grace* as well as truth (*John* 1:14). Augustine remarked that love can communicate where language does not.[8] William Penn wrote in 1692:[9]

> *It is not opinion, or speculation, or notions of what is true,*
> *or assent to or the subscription of articles or propositions,*
> *though never so soundly worded, that . . . makes a man*

a true believer or a true Christian. But it is a conformity
of mind to the will of God, in all holiness of conversation,
according to the dictates of this Divine principle of Light
and Life in the soul which denotes a person truly a child
of God.[10]

Experiencing the divine Light thus involves affective responses
that are part of an ongoing transformation of the self. But any
claimed mystical or "enthusiastic" experiences in which "the presence of God" or "the power of the Spirit" is putatively felt need
to be tested by their integration into ongoing experience and behavior, within and outside the religious community. Quakers or
other religious "enthusiasts" had better not propose to replace a
doctrine of infallible church or scripture by one of infallible individual experience, tempting as that may be to some. The experience of a "gathered" Quaker meeting can be understood as
a *collective* awareness of divine presence, a group mystical experience.[11] But even that needs testing by further discernment, for
any group can be led astray.

But can one "do" spirituality without "doing" God? Many people,
including some Quakers, now think so. That raises the question of
what conception of God they are *rejecting*. And confirms my suspicion that there is much confusion about the matter, which I hope
this little book might help clarify. Quakerism arose within (and in
reaction to) seventeenth-century Christianity in Britain, and now
has three and a half centuries of tradition behind it. *Quaker Faith
and Practice* is a compilation of writings over that time, occasionally

revised. Its first chapter is the *Advices and Queries*, a set of 42 carefully worded short paragraphs, setting out the Quaker way of life
and its spiritual basis in brief compass. These "Advices" mention
God,[12] Christ, and the Holy Spirit, so there is a faint vestige of
Trinitarian theology.[13] Early Quakers described the inward Light
as the light of Christ, echoing *John* 8:12—"I am the light of the
world. No follower of mine shall walk in darkness; he shall have
the light of life." There is similar talk of the Holy Spirit in *John*
14:16–17, 15:26, 16:13–15. This need not imply any perception
of the Spirit in physical form but rather a *means* by which we are
enabled to perceive spiritual truths and live up to them.

Religious traditions and theologies are not timeless: they
change and develop, for better or for worse. In recent years
some British Quakers have become reluctant to talk of God at all
and have labeled themselves "non-theists." In 1985 John Lampen
proposed a very flexible interpretation of language about God:

> *To apply the term "God" (in the Christian sense) is
> to say that we perceive intuitively a connection be-
> tween the marvels of the natural world, the moral law,
> the life of Jesus, the depths of the human personality,
> our imaginations about time, death and eternity, our
> experiences of human forgiveness and love, and the
> finest insights of the Christian tradition. To deny the ex-
> istence of "God" is to say that we cannot (yet) see such
> connections. But even the word "God" is not an essential
> tool for grasping them.[14]*

That fits with my tentative discussion of forgiveness and grace in the previous Chapter. It is not the *word* or *concept* "God" but the experienced spiritual reality that is vital. *Advices and Queries* no.8 reads:

> *Worship is our response to an awareness of God. We can*
> *worship alone, but when we join with others in expectant*
> *waiting we may discover a deeper sense of God's presence.*
> *We seek a gathered stillness in our meetings for worship*
> *so that all may feel the power of God's love drawing us*
> *together and leading us.* [15]

I feel more certainty about the truth of these sentences *taken as wholes*, i.e., about the reality of God's presence and the power of his love, than about the precise reference of the G-word considered in isolation. [16] The former is a matter of religious experience and practice, but the latter is a conceptual puzzle eternally debated in theology and philosophy, as surveyed in Part I. I suggest one can accept that these phrases as expressing experienced spiritual realities, while being somewhat vague about what the putative name "God" refers to. [17] This may be the condition of millions of religious adherents, not only Quakers, and dare I suggest that it need not be intellectually or spiritually bankrupt?

There are analogies for this relaxed interpretation of nouns in the use of nominalization and personification in poetry. Consider Shakespeare's Sonnet LX:

Like as the waves make towards the pebbled shore,
So do our minutes hasten to their end;

Each changing place with that which goes before,
In sequent toil all forwards do contend.
Nativity, once in the main of light,
Crawls to maturity, wherewith being crown'd,
Crooked eclipses 'gainst his glory fight,
And Time that gave doth now his gift confound.

Here the abstract noun "nativity" is a synonym for "infancy," and when nativity is said to crawl that is obviously a poetic figure of speech for what infants do, and being crowned with "maturity" means growing up to adulthood. "Time" is capitalized and personified, as so often in Shakespeare: in this poem "Time" first gives life and later mars or takes away his gift. There is, of course, no such *person* as Time, though Lewis Carroll made a logical joke when Alice was told by the Mad Hatter: "He won't stand beating!" If the word "thing" is taken as referring to an identifiable object or substance, then there is no such *thing* as Time (as Augustine famously noted in his *Confessions*). But time certainly passes, with the ravages and deaths that it brings, as Shakespeare so mordantly sings. The word "Time" does not really function as a name (even when capitalized), but the passage of time is an unavoidable and poignant reality of human life.

Consider also the personification of Love in George Herbert's much-loved poem:

LOVE bade me welcome; yet my soul drew back,
Guilty of dust and sin.
But quick-eyed Love, observing me grow slack

From my first entrance in,
Drew nearer to me, sweetly questioning
If I lack'd anything.

Here only literal-minded philosophers (or literary critics?) will
stop to remark on the conceptual absurdity of an abstraction
"Love" doing the welcoming, observing, and questioning: the rest
of us can easily accept it as a figure of speech. This is obviously
a religious poem, and "Love" can readily be understood as God,
or Christ, or the Trinity—even perhaps as Yahweh or Allah? In
Herbert's second stanza "Love" is represented as creator ("who
made the eyes"), and in the third as redeemer ("who bore the
blame"). But the spiritual meaning of the poem does not depend
on any particular metaphysical conception of God, creation, or
atonement.

This is a point where I can appropriate some of the insights
of the Wittgensteinian interpretation of Christianity reviewed in
Chapter 13. Moore said, like Tillich, that the word "God" is not
the name of somebody, not even a heavenly, spiritual person or
thing. But he suggested that we can establish the *presence* of God by
seeing a man saying his prayers, and nothing else. That appeared
to reduce the presence of God to a certain kind of human activity,
but perhaps a better interpretation is that when we pray (or participate in a Quaker Meeting for Worship), we do not literally see
or hear a being called "God" yet there is a sense in which sincere
prayer brings us *into* a spiritual state which deserves the title "the

presence of God." It is not like being ushered into the physical presence of the Queen, more like contemplating one's smallness compared to the universe in space and time and one's imperfection when judged by the highest standards.[18]

For most of us it is not that the name "God" is first given reference to a mysterious imperceptible transcendent being, and we are then exhorted to develop the attitudes appropriate to such an extraordinary entity; but rather, the relevant attitudes, dispositions and activities are what give *sense* to belief in God. Religion is part of a form of life, it is practice more than theory. The eternally debated question whether God exists is not so much a factual yet mysteriously unresolvable hypothesis about the existence of some extremely elusive entity, but rather a decision to adopt talk and thought of God into our practice because that way of interpreting our lives is seen as appropriate, fitting, inspiring— and in the deepest sense realistic.[19]

AN "UNCONCLUDING" APPENDIX

I prefer to call this an appendix rather than a conclusion, because on matters of religion and theology, where traditions, experiences, tastes, and convictions differ so sharply, what conclusions anyone can offer cannot be conclusive. So I invite the reader to join me in remaining open to new light, wherever it comes from.[1]

Part I touched on rational arguments for the existence and nature of God in classic thinkers and recently in David Bentley Hart, touching on a more nuanced mixture of rationalism, empiricism, morality, and spirituality in the works of Keith Ward. The latter has admitted in one place that "the limits of rational theology verge on fantasy, and, as our normal concepts begin to break and fall away, we find ourselves in a logical vacuum where reason and imagination become confused"—and that's a rational theologian speaking! For Ward the borderland of fantasy came at talk of angels and archangels, on which he piously or circumspectly suggested we had better embrace "the silence of wisdom" and "bow down before God's incomprehensibility."

But for many, including myself, the limits of rational theology are encountered much earlier, with the danger of it becoming an intellectual game for academics and enthusiasts to play, apparently arguing about mysterious matters of metaphysical fact but missing the point of religious faith and practice. This motivated my review of various species of non-realism in Part II, where I concluded that some rather elusive dimension of realism, objectivity, and truth is needed if religion is not to be a completely arbitrary and culturally relative matter.

There is more than enough religious dogmatism in the world, and I have no wish to add to it. I suggest there is wisdom in leaving things open-ended, even somewhat vague. The Quaker astronomer Arthur Eddington expressed this attitude eloquently in 1929:

> *Rejection of creed is not inconsistent with being possessed by a living belief. We have no creed in science, but we are not lukewarm in our beliefs. The belief is not that all the knowledge of the universe that we hold so enthusiastically will survive in the letter; but a sureness that we are on the road. If our so-called facts are changing shadows, they are shadows cast by the light of constant truth. So too in religion we are repelled by that confident theological doctrine which has settled for all generations just how the spiritual world is worked; but we need not turn aside from the measure of light that comes into our experience showing us a Way through the unseen world. Religion for the conscientious seeker is not all a matter of doubt and self-questionings. There is a kind of sureness which is very different from cocksureness.* [2]

For most adherents of the various religions, faith consists more in religious practice, a "Way" rather than belief in a set of metaphysical propositions. I suggest we can feel quietly confident that we are on the right road and that we have been given sufficient Light to proceed down it, without tying ourselves dogmatically to particular creedal formulas or theological theories about the nature of God.

NOTES

Chapter 1

1. I have added italics in these quotations to emphasize the bodily imagery they involve.
2. There is a strange little fragment at *Genesis* 6:1–5 (hardly consistent with the rest of the Hebrew Bible) in which the Nephilim, the "sons of gods," are said to have had intercourse with "the daughters of mortals." It looks as if a bit of pagan mythology was inadvertently included by the ancient editors.
3. For example, "Aeneas whom the radiant Aphrodite bore Anchises down the folds of Ida, a goddess bedded with a man" in the *Iliad* 2:931–2, translated by Robert Fagles (Viking Penguin, 1990). There is a sympathetic account of the ancient Greek gods as symbols in Chapter 1 of Keith Ward, *God: A Guide for the Perplexed* (Oneworld, 2001).
4. The *Ghent Altar-piece* by Jan van Eyck (a fifteenth-century genius of the northern Renaissance) shows a red-robed regal male enthroned in the prime of life. Opinions differ whether this was intended to represent God the Father, Christ in majesty, or the Trinity—the latter may be indicated by the tripartite structure of his headgear.
5. Was it thought that two-dimensional paintings could get around the biblical prohibition of three-dimensional "graven" images, i.e., sculptures or bas-reliefs?
6. "Elohim" (a plural) is one of the words for God in the beginning of the Hebrew scriptures. Blake formed his idiosyncratic mythology and iconography from biblical sources.
7. At *Exodus* 19:20 we are told that the Lord came down on the top of Mount Sinai, yet at *I Kings* 8:27 we read: "But can God indeed dwell on earth? Heaven itself, the highest heaven, cannot contain you; how much

less this house that I have built!" These texts from different periods may show development in the Hebrew idea of God; the first would need to be given a nonliteral interpretation to avoid the implication that God moves through space.

8. Ludwig Wittgenstein, *Lectures and Conversations on Aesthetics, Psychology and Religious Belief* (Blackwell, 1966), p. 63.

9. See David Cecil, *Visionary and Dreamer: Two Poetic Painters: Samuel Palmer and Edward Burne-Jones* (Constable, 1969). A poetic version of Palmer's vision of nature can perhaps be found in the creation prayers and hymns of the ancient Celtic brand of Christianity that was edged out of most of Britain after the Synod of Whitby in the year 664. For example:

> *The grace of the love of the skies be thine,*
> *The grace of the love of the stars be thine,*
> *The grace of the love of the moon be thine,*
> *The grace of the love of the sun be thine.*

From the *Carmina Gadelica* III, ed. Alexander Carmichael (Scottish Academic Press, 1976), p. 233, quoted by Philip Newell in *Heartbeat of God: A Celtic Spirituality* (SPCK, 1997), p. 42. In the nineteenth century Carmichael collected fragments of the oral Celtic tradition still surviving in the Hebrides and west coast of Scotland despite the disapproval of schoolmasters and Kirk ministers.

Chapter 2

1. I have added italics in these quotations to emphasize the mental states they ascribe to God.

2. In his chapter in *The Openness of God: A Biblical Challenge to the Traditional Understanding of God* (InterVarsity Press, 1994), p. 35, Richard Rice insists that the biblical talk of God's thoughts and feelings is to be understood literally, unlike the talk of his physical embodiment.

3. Richard Swinburne, *The Coherence of Theism* (Oxford University Press, 1979), p. 1. He set out his views in more compact form in *Is There a God?* (Oxford University Press, 1996), where on p. 2 he declared: "The

very same criteria which scientists use to reach their own theories lead us to move beyond those theories to a creator God who sustains everything in existence," and on p. 139 he concluded that the various kinds of evidence that we have "all make it significantly more probable than not that there is a God." But I share the common reaction that science and religion involve quite different criteria for belief, and that a God whose existence is seen only as "more probable than not" can hardly be the God of religious faith. See the discussion of Kant on faith in Chapter 14.

4. Alvin Plantinga, *Warranted Christian Belief* (Oxford University Press, 2000), Preface. In that lengthy magnum opus, Plantinga offers a quite different intellectual defense of Christian belief from Swinburne's, arguing that it does not depend on or need empirical evidence but is "warranted" (adequately justified) by a kind of internal conviction inspired or "instigated" in us by the Holy Spirit. (But what becomes of those in whom the Holy Spirit does not seem to work?—Does this imply that God "elects" or predestines some of us for salvation and condemns others irrespective of what we believe and do?) Plantinga's strategy seems to *assume* the truth of some portion of Christian belief (notably the operation of the Holy Spirit) and that has laid him open to a charge of circularity, since his defense of Christianity "from within" seems to show only that those who already accept it can be internally "warranted" in retaining that belief.

5. God tends to be identified as male even if not embodied. Feminist theologians ask why an incorporeal person should be gendered (either way). No pronoun—"he" or "she" or "it"—feels quite right for God.

6. That genial Edwardian English existentialist (if there can be such a thing).

7. G. K. Chesterton, *Orthodoxy* (Hodder & Stoughton, 1996; first published 1908), p. 89.

8. Sallie McFague, *Metaphorical Theology* (SCM Press, 1982), p. 128.

9. Nicholas Lash, *Easter in Ordinary* (SCM Press, 1988), p. 276.

10. See notes 2 and 3, this chapter.

Chapter 3

1. For an easy introduction to Aristotle see Chapter 5 in Leslie Stevenson et al., *Thirteen Theories of Human Nature*, 7th ed. (Oxford University Press, 2017). For a comprehensive survey of his thought see the online *Stanford Encyclopedia of Philosophy* article.

2. Aristotle, *Physics* VII, *Metaphysics* XII.6.

3. For a comprehensive survey of his thought see the online *Stanford Encyclopedia of Philosophy* article on Ibn Sina (Avicenna).

4. For a comprehensive survey of Maimonides's thought see the online *Stanford Encyclopedia of Philosophy* article.

5. Maimonides, *Guide of the Perplexed*, Book II, Chapters XIII–XXVII.

6. Maimonides, Book I, Chapters XXXV, LII, LIV; Book III, Chapter XX.

7. Maimonides, Book I, Chapter LVIII. See the next chapter for some discussion of apophatic theology.

8. For a comprehensive survey of Aquinas's thought see the online *Stanford Encyclopedia of Philosophy* article.

9. Aquinas, *Summa theologiae*, I.13.5.

10. Aquinas, *Summa theologiae*, I.1.1 and I.1.10.

11. Aquinas, *Summa theologiae*, I.3.1–8.

12. For example Brian Davies, "A Modern Defense of the Classical Doctrine of God's Simplicity," Chapter 52 in Brian Davies, *Language, Meaning and God* (Geoffrey Chapman, 1987). Davies practically identifies the doctrine of simplicity with the apophatic denial that we can know anything positive of God.

13. Keith Ward, *Christ and the Cosmos* (Cambridge University Press, 2015), pp. 13, 15. Ward here seems to assume that theology is in the business of *explanation*, which raises the question of how it relates to science.

14. Aquinas, *Summa theologiae*, I.2.3.

15. David Bentley Hart, *The Experience of God: Being, Consciousness, Bliss* (Yale University Press, 2013), p. 30.

16. Hart, *The Experience of God*, p. 286.

17. Hart, *The Experience of God*, p. 28.

18. Iris Murdoch (a novelist, and not a conventional theist) wrote "Metaphors are not merely peripheral decorations or even useful

models. They are fundamental forces of our awareness of our condition," see *The Sovereignty of Good* (Routledge, 1970), p. 77.

19. Hart, *The Experience of God*, p. 147.
20. Hart, *The Experience of God*, p. 294.
21. Kant, *Critique of Pure Reason* (1781), A603–14/B631–42. In his "precritical" period twenty years earlier Kant defended his own sophisticated version of the argument for the existence of a necessary being.
22. Kant, *Critique of Pure Reason*, A609/B637.
23. For more on Kant see Chapter 16.
24. Kant, *Critique of Pure Reason*, A619/B647. See Essay 5 of my *Inspirations from Kant* (Oxford University Press, 2011) for further discussion of these themes.
25. Hart, *The Experience of God*, p. 320. Keith Ward suggests that Aquinas's "Five Ways" can be read not so much as philosophical arguments but as exercises in meditation, see *God: A Guide for the Perplexed* (Oneworld, 2001), pp. 54–5.
26. Hart, *The Experience of God*, p. 44.
27. Hart, *The Experience of God*, pp. 314–15.

Chapter 4

1. Heidegger's opaque thought is not explicitly atheist like Sartre's, and some theologians have found it sympathetic, but he resisted any identification of "Being" with God as conventionally understood. For a stimulating introduction see George Steiner, *Heidegger* (Fontana/Collins, 1978).
2. The mysterious title arose because this early medieval writer represented himself as Dionysius, a member of the Council of the Greek Areopagus mentioned at *Acts* 17:34 as converted to Christianity by St. Paul. For a comprehensive survey see the online *Stanford Encyclopedia of Philosophy* article on Dionysius.
3. John Scottus Eriugena (ca. 800–877) was the first Irish philosopher of note before George Berkey in the early eighteenth century (Berkeley propounded a different theistic system, arguing that God's perception maintains everything in existence when not perceived by us). In

Eriugena's times, conventionally described as "the dark ages," Ireland was known as "the island of saints and scholars, and its inhabitants of were called 'Scotti.'" His example shows that the intellectual "darkness" of Europe was not complete. For a comprehensive survey of his thought see the online *Stanford Encyclopedia of Philosophy* article on Eriugena. On his contribution to the Celtic tradition of Christian spirituality that emphasized God's presence in the whole of creation see Philip Newell, *Heartbeat of God* (SPCK, 1997).

4. Eckhardt von Hochheim OP (ca. 1260–1328) was a theological graduate of the University of Paris and a member of the Dominican Order. For a comprehensive survey see the online *Stanford Encyclopedia of Philosophy*. Late in his life the Inquisition put him on trial, and some of his theses were condemned as heretical, but he died before the matter could be concluded. Religious authorities seem to find it difficult to tolerate apophatic theology; they tend to require clarity about religious identity and loyalty to defining dogmas. Socrates, Spinoza, and Kant also got into trouble for their interpretations of religion, as have some Islamic philosophers.

5. David Bentley Hart, *The Experience of God: Being, Consciousness, Bliss* (Yale University Press, 2013), p. 142.

6. William James, *The Varieties of Religious Experience: A Study in Human Nature,* Gifford Lectures delivered at Edinburgh in 1901–2 (Collins, 1960).

Chapter 5

1. The *Wisdom of Solomon* is in the *Apocrypha*, a set of books not included in the authoritative canon of the Jews but often printed between the Old and New Testaments in Christian Bibles. (There is even disagreement about which writings should be included in the *Apocrypha*.) The *Wisdom of Solomon* is not thought to have been written by King Solomon but by an Alexandrian Jew who was well-versed in both Jewish and Greek thought. It seems there was some limited interaction between those two very different ancient cultures.

2. For an easy introduction to Plato's thought see Chapter 5 in Leslie Stevenson et al., *Thirteen Theories of Human Nature*, 7th ed. (Oxford University Press, 2017). For a comprehensive survey see the online *Stanford Encyclopedia of Philosophy* article on Plato.

3. Plato, *Republic* 514–19.

4. Plato, *Symposium* 204–12.

5. Plato, *Republic* 472–514.

6. See especially Augustine's *Confessions* and *On Free Choice of the Will*. The influence of Plato on Augustine was strong but indirect, through the third century Neo-Platonist philosopher Plotinus.

7. *On Free Choice of the Will*, Chapter Two, sections 6–15. This dialogue was written soon after Augustine's conversion to Christianity and may not represent his more mature conclusions. See John M. Rist, *Augustine* (Cambridge University Press, 1994), pp. 67–71; and Scott Macdonald, "The Divine Nature," Chapter 6 in *The Cambridge Companion to Augustine*, ed. E. Stump and N. Kretzmann (Cambridge University Press, 2001), pp. 71–90.

8. David Bentley Hart, *The Experience of God: Being, Consciousness, Bliss* (Yale University Press, 2013).

9. Hart, *The Experience of God*, pp. 233–5.

10. Hart, *The Experience of God*, p. 250.

11. William Kingdom Clifford, "The Ethics of Belief," *Contemporary Review* 1877.

12. Hart, *The Experience of God*, pp. 251–4.

13. Hart, *The Experience of God*, pp. 256, 274.

14. Hart, *The Experience of God*, pp. 283–4.

15. There are surely different kinds of truth in different domains. Mathematical truths are necessarily true and are knowable a priori (i.e., without appeal to perception of the material world). Contingent claims about the world have to be justified empirically by perception (directly or indirectly), but laws of nature are universal generalizations, and have a different sort of truth, for they are not facts about particular objects and events. If we recognize objective moral truths, they must have a different status. And aesthetic truths, if there are such things, would be different again.

16. Keith Ward, *God: A Guide for the Perplexed* (Oneworld, 2001), pp. 215–16, 198.
17. Iris Murdoch, *The Sovereignty of Good* (Routledge, 1970), p. 55. To my mind, this fifty-year-old slim volume is one of the most inspiring works of moral philosophy and philosophy of religion.
18. Murdoch, *The Sovereignty of Good*, p. 74. Compare also Kant's conception of "moral faith," discussed in Chapter 16.
19. Murdoch, *The Sovereignty of Good*, p. 79. In her later book *Metaphysics as a Guide to Morals* (Chatto & Windus, 1992), Murdoch left us with a much lengthier, somewhat wandering, but thought-provoking meditation on similar themes. A one-sentence summary might be: "Good represents the reality of which God is the dream" (p. 496).

Chapter 6

1. For an introduction see Roger Scruton, *Spinoza* (Oxford University Press, 1986). For a comprehensive discussion see the online *Stanford Encyclopedia of Philosophy* article.
2. Expounded systematically in Spinoza's *Theological-Political Treatise*, published clandestinely in Amsterdam in 1669–1670; edited with a helpful introduction by Jonathan Israel (Cambridge University Press, 2007). After extensive discussion of prophecy, miracles, and the historical and theological interpretation of scripture, Spinoza concluded the work with a classic early-modern defense of freedom of thought and publication in a democratic law-governed society. He aimed to undercut the power of religious authorities, so one early critic accordingly called it a book "forged in hell by the devil himself"!
3. The full title is *Ethics: Proved in Geometrical Order*, first published posthumously in 1677. This book is extremely difficult to read even for professional philosophers; however when Spinoza departs from his formal apparatus of definitions, axioms, propositions, and proofs and gives us a bit of continuous prose, his views emerge more clearly. On his conception of God see especially the Appendix to Part I.
4. Spinoza, *Ethics*, Part I, Proposition XVII, Note.
5. Spinoza, *Ethics*, Part I, Appendix.

6. Spinoza, *Ethics*, Part I, Appendix.

7. David Hume, *A Treatise of Human Nature* (1739), I.iv.v. Later in the eighteenth century there arose a famous "pantheism controversy" within German intellectual culture, ostensibly about whether Lessing (a key figure in the German Enlightenment) had adhered to Spinozist pantheism. But the real issue at stake was the implications of applying reason to religion—which is still a live issue for us all. See the general introduction to Immanuel Kant, *Religion and Rational Theology*, translated and edited by Allen W. Wood and George di Giovanni (Cambridge University Press, 1996).

8. See the 2013 Sanders Lecture by R. M. Adams at https://vimeo.com/91335367.

9. For an introduction to Freud's thought see Chapter 10 in Leslie Stevenson et al., *Thirteen Theories of Human Nature*, 7th ed. (Oxford University Press, 2017).

10. For an easy introduction see Peter Singer, *Hegel* (Oxford University Press, 1983). For a comprehensive survey of his thought see the online *Stanford Encyclopedia of Philosophy* article. I am not attempting more than a one-paragraph summary of Hegel's wordy and opaque philosophy.

11. Bacteria and ferns, fishes and amphibians, dinosaurs and hominids preceded the evolution of human life, which we tend complacently to see as the main purpose of the whole story. Maybe the dinosaurs were a spectacular but unnecessary sideshow, for we have evolved from mammals, not reptiles. But now astronomers are detecting other planets that may house intelligent creatures who might be moral and spiritual in their own way. So if we are debating the purpose of the universe, Hegel's philosophy of "Absolute Spirit" (or any other theology of God's providence) had better apply to all evolutions of life wherever they have transpired.

12. For a sympathetic review of Hegel's conception of God as involved in the development of the world through time, see Chapter 5 of Keith Ward, *God: A Guide for the Perplexed* (Oneworld, 2001). Ward sounds more persuaded than me about the idea of a final divine consummation of history.

Chapter 7

1. Plato's dialogue the *Timaeus* presents an elaborate pre-Christian account of the creation of the universe, in which a benevolent but not omnipotent craftsman or "demiurge" uses the existing material as best he can, trying to make it conform to the ideal standards set by the Platonic Forms. This can count as deism, since the demiurge (a "god" with a small "g") is not represented as doing anything afterward.

2. After Voltaire's death came the French Revolution of 1789, and in its violent aftermath Robespierre tried to replace Catholicism with a new "Cult of the Supreme Being," only to be guillotined himself in 1794—though not, as I understand it, for deism. English deists usually died in their beds, though in 1791 the scientist and unitarian Joseph Priestley was forced by a mob to flee his house in Birmingham and later emigrated to America. It seems that religious non-conformity and support for the French Revolution were equally suspect in England at that time.

3. Many of these figures were also Unitarians, holding the closely associated view that rejected the doctrine of the Trinity and insisted on the unity of God. Some of them, Thomas Paine at least, retained belief in individual life after death.

4. See the official website: deism.com.

5. Even that has been described by tough-minded philosophers as epistemic irresponsibility, a kind of intellectual sin, most famously by W. K. Clifford in "The Ethics of Belief," *Contemporary Review* 1877.

6. The fiery second- to third-century Christian theologian Tertullian is reported as saying, "I believe *because* it is absurd," though that was perhaps a mere rhetorical flourish. Many centuries later Kierkegaard made a more definite appeal to absurdity and paradox in his radically existential characterization of Christian faith (see Chapter 16, note 13).

7. For an introduction to Darwin and some neo-Darwinian theories of human nature see Chapter 12 in Leslie Stevenson et al., *Thirteen Theories of Human Nature*, 7th ed. (Oxford University Press, 2017).

8. Maurice Wiles, *God's Action in the World* (SCM Press, 1986).

9. Keith Ward, *Divine Action: Examining God's Role in an Open and Emergent Universe* (Templeton Foundation Press, 2007; first published by Flame in 1990).

Chapter 8

1. Plato, *Sophist* 247e.
2. God can still be described as omniscient in the more limited sense that *at any given time* he knows all the facts that hold at that time.
3. The latter option assumes that the future of the universe is *not* predetermined (as was suggested by naïve but popular generalizations from Newtonian mechanics), but is in some ways genuinely open and unpredictable, due to quantum indeterminacies or human free will or both. See Keith Ward, *Divine Action: Examining God's Role in an Open and Emergent Universe* (Templeton Foundation Press, 2007). See also my own argument against determinism in the last chapter of *Inspirations from Kant* (Oxford University Press, 2011), or the revised version entitled "Who's Afraid of Determinism?" in *Philosophy* 2014.
4. As Aquinas put it: "Nothing can come into contact with God or partially intermingle with him in any way," *Summa theologiae*, 1.13.5.
5. Open theism is argued for in detail by Clark H. Pinnock, Richard Rice, John Sanders, William Hasker, and David Basinger in *The Openness of God: A Biblical Challenge to the Traditional Understanding of God* (InterVarsity Press, 1994), also in Clark Pinnock, *Most Moved Mover: A Theology of God's Openness* (Baker Academic, 2001).
6. Open theism differs from the "process theology" derived from the metaphysical philosophy of A. N. Whitehead (1861–1947), in which change is the fundamental category of everything; God and world being interdependent parts of the whole process. Open theism insists in more biblical fashion that God is independent of the world yet acts in it.
7. Keith Ward, *Rational Theology and the Creativity of God* (Blackwell, 1982), pp. 80–1, 151, 220. See also Chapter 5 of his *God: A Guide for the Perplexed* (Oneworld, 2001).
8. Most of the biblical stories of God-given pregnancies seem open to either interpretation. But the case of the impregnation of the Virgin Mary by the Holy Ghost is miraculous in the stronger sense of not involving a human male in insemination.
9. Or as someone has mysteriously put it: "God acts in his creature's acting by causing it to be the cause that it is." The doctrine of divine concurrence is attributed to Aquinas, Suarez, and Leibniz. See Christopher J.

Insole, *Kant and the Creation of Freedom: A Theological Problem* (Oxford University Press, 2013), p. 10. The whole book is a deep and difficult treatment of this idea.

10. Austin Farrer, *Faith and Speculation: An Essay in Philosophical Theology* (A and C Black, 1967).

11. Ward, *Divine Action*, pp. 36, 74, 77, 109, 119, 123, 127, 141, 171, 236.

12. Ward, *Divine Action*, pp. 55, 196.

13. The practical implications of open theism outlined by David Basinger in the concluding chapter of *The Openness of God* (note 5 in this chapter) include the practice of petitionary prayer, conventionally understood as asking God to do things. This assumes that God gets to hear a prayer at a certain time, and then decides whether to answer it by an intervention in the world that he might not otherwise have performed. Open theism makes this intelligible, but is open to the familiar complaint that God often does not seem to answer prayers for intervention even in extreme cases of human suffering and evildoing.

14. The strictest Calvinist has to recognize that human beings make decisions, even if those decisions are predestined in God's complete plan for the history of the world.

15. For an introduction to Marx's thought see Chapter 9 in Leslie Stevenson et al., *Thirteen Theories of Human Nature*, 7th ed. (Oxford University Press, 2017).

16. Pierre Teilhard de Chardin, *The Phenomenon of Man* (Sussex Academic, 2003). Teilhard's bold cosmic theorizing came under theological suspicion, and he was forbidden by his Jesuit superiors to persist in it. But it has been more positively received (posthumously) by Popes John Paul II and Benedict XVI.

17. At the other extreme from Teilhard, the idea of progress has been stringently criticized by the prolific English political philosopher John Gray in a series of eloquently (and sarcastically) written books including *Straw Dogs: Thoughts on Human and Other Animals* (Granta Books, 2002) and *Seven Types of Atheism* (Allen Lane, 2018). He argues that the "liberal" faith in human progress through history (characteristic of the Enlightenment in Kant and above all in Hegel, widespread even now) is a secular hangover of religious faith in God's providence. Gray has no time for the latter, and delights in punching holes in the former

with detailed and often disturbing examples of the variety of human cultures, religions and politics, with no guarantee of a better "more liberal" future. Yet he still endorses liberal *values*, at least half-heartedly, when he writes "a liberal way of life is one of the more civilized ways in which human beings can live together" even though there is no providential guidance for the future of *societies* in which liberal values are recognized (*Seven Types of Atheism*, p. 93).

18. Open theism has come under attack for questioning God's omnipotence and omniscience. It has been defended by Tomas Jay Oord in *The Uncontrolling Love of God* (InterVarsity Press, 2015), who has himself been accused of heresy by defenders of the classic impassable conception of God.

19. Of course Jewish and Christian theologians cite their preferred passages and preferred interpretations of the Bible as authoritative, and Muslims similarly appeal to the Qur'an. But on the question of God's temporality (as on various other issues such as the legitimacy of slavery, and the equality of men and women), the scriptures seem to point both ways, and many interpreters can find some text somewhere to try to back themselves up with sacred authority.

20. For example: "God Is a Risk-Taker," *The Openness of God*, p. 151.

21. *The Openness of God*, p. 154.

Chapter 9

1. Michael Leunig, *The Lot: In Words* (Penguin Group Australia, 2008), p. 234; quoted by Rowan Williams in *The Edge of Words* (Bloomsbury, 2014), p. 4.

2. R. B. Braithwaite, *An Empiricist's Account of the Nature of Religious Belief* (Cambridge University Press, 1955).

Chapter 10

1. Ludwig Feuerbach, *The Essence of Christianity*, translated by George Eliot—the famous nineteenth century novelist (Prometheus Books, 1989). Page references in parentheses in this chapter are to this edition.

2. Don Cupitt, *Taking Leave of God* (SCM Press, 1980), pp. 102–3, 106.
3. Don Cupitt, *The Sea of Faith* (Cambridge University Press, 1984), p. 269.
4. The figure of Britannia personified Britain's erstwhile naval power on old-fashioned pre-decimal pennies, and in the song "Britannia Rules the Waves" still sung on the last night of the London proms.
5. Don Cupitt, *Philosophy's Own Religion* (SCM Press, 2000), footnote on p. 170. A similar view was presented by a former Anglican priest Anthony Freeman, when he wrote: "Now I have decided to change my use of the term 'God.' Instead of referring it to a supernatural being, I shall apply it to the sum of all my values and ideals in life" in *God in Us: A Case for Christian Humanism* (Imprint Academic, 1993), p. 19. That led to Freeman being dismissed from his parish for contravening church teaching: even "broad church" Anglicanism sometimes sets theological limits.
6. You can get "God" and "sake" into a single sentence such as "Do it now, for God's sake!"
7. The nouns "whereabouts" and "aegis" are similar linguistic oddities in English.

Chapter 11

1. Other interpretations of Kant have emphasized the "empirical realism" that he also propounded, namely his recognition (against Berkeley) of the mind-independent existence of the material world, notwithstanding his elusive and controversial "transcendental idealism." See my *Inspirations from Kant* (Oxford University Press, 2011).
2. Don Cupitt, *The Sea of Faith* (Cambridge University Press, 1984), p. 20; *Creation Out of Nothing* (SCM Press, 1990), pp. 68, 81, 85.
3. Don Cupitt, *Creation Out of Nothing* (SCM Press, 1990), pp. 152–3.
4. Cupitt, *The Sea of Faith* (Cambridge University Press, 1984), pp. 270–1.
5. These semantic matters are very slippery and are the subject of infinite subtleties in the philosophy of language.
6. In *Philosophy's Own Religion* (SCM Press, 2000), Cupitt invoked a whiff of Heideggerian mysticism: "Apart from our input, apart from

our language, there is only non-language, which is formless, ineffable Being" (p. 56).

7. "It is totally false to suggest that deconstruction is a suspension of reference . . . to distance oneself from the habitual structure of reference, to challenge or complicate our common assumptions about it, does not amount to saying that there is nothing beyond language." quoted by Daphne Hampson in *God and Reality: Essays on Christian Non-realism*, ed. Colin Crowder (Mowbray, 1997).

8. Peter Byrne has done an effective demolition job on non-realism in general and in theology, and I do not need to labor the point further here. See his *God and Realism* (Ashgate, 2003).

Chapter 12

1. Alan Keightley presented a useful critical survey of the philosophies of religion of Ludwig Wittgenstein, in Rush Rhees, Peter Winch, and D. Z. Phillips, eds., *Wittgenstein, Grammar and God* (Epworth Press, 1976).

2. It is a remarkable sociological fact that religious beliefs (at least on traditional definitions) are now absent from large segments of European populations but still prevalent in the United States and in most of the rest of the world.

3. See Terry Eagleton, *The Meaning of Life* (Oxford University Press, 2007), and André Comte-Sponville, *The Book of Atheist Spirituality* (Bantam Press, 2007).

4. Paul Tillich made a serious, if rather wordy, effort in this direction in *The Courage to Be*, 3rd. ed. (Yale University Press, 2014).

Chapter 13

1. Phillips's first book, *The Concept of Prayer* (Routledge and Kegan Paul, 1965), is an unusual combination of philosophy and spirituality, strongly influenced by Kierkegaard and by Simone Weil. See also his collection of essays *Recovering Religious Concepts* (Macmillan Press, 2000).

2. Gareth Moore, *Believing in God* (T&T Clark, 1988); numbers in parentheses in this chapter refer to this book.
3. To which Aquinas belonged seven centuries earlier.
4. Moore makes a passing reference to Meister Eckhart's apophatic theology on pp. 158–60.
5. Even child abuse, and the Holocaust, one wonders?—the problem of evil rears its ugly head again. See the discussion in Chapter 8.
6. This is a main theme of D. Z. Phillips's *oeuvre*.
7. On pp. 79–80 Moore quotes the pioneering anthropologist Evans-Pritchard who claimed to have become similarly acculturated when he lived amongst the Azande in Africa in the 1930s.

Chapter 14

1. Rudolf Otto, *The Idea of the Holy: An Inquiry into the Non-Rational Factor in the Idea of the Divine and Its Relation to the Rational*, translated by John W. Harvey (Pelican, 1959). Numbers in parentheses in this chapter refer to pages of this edition.
2. William James's famous Gifford Lectures of 1902, *The Varieties of Religious Experience*, subtitled "A Study in Human Nature" (Fontana, 1960), constitute another detailed study of the psychology of religious experiences. James is interested in their variety, whereas Otto claims to discern a common core, and is more concerned with the objects of religious experience, the apprehension of some sort of reality.
3. For example David Bentley Hart, as noted in Chapter 4.
4. When Kant talked of a holy will, he meant a disposition or character that always conforms to the moral law.
5. *The Bhagavad Gita*, translated by Gavin Flood and Charles Martin (W. W. Norton, 2015), 11.9–10, 18, 25. This ancient text expresses a strand of personal monotheism within the many varieties of Hinduism. For an introduction to Hinduism see Chapter 2 by David Haberman in Leslie Stevenson et al., *Thirteen Theories of Human Nature*, 7th ed. (Oxford University Press, 2017).
6. *Critique of Judgment*, 5:314. Kant did not evince any particular sensitivity to music, but he did remark that "music, which is a regular play

of aural sensations, not only moves sense in a way that is indescribably vivacious and varied, but also strengthens it; for music is as it were a language of sheer sensations (without any concepts)" (*Anthropology*, 7:155). In his third *Critique* Kant had a puzzling theory that aesthetic experience involves a "free play" between our faculties of imagination and understanding (*Critique of Judgment*, 5:240–1, 287, 316–17, 354). I touched on this mysterious theme in my essay "Twelve Conceptions of Imagination," *British Journal of Aesthetics* 2003.

7. John Muir, the Scottish-born ecologist and conservationist who inspired the national parks movement in the United States, wrote: "the charms of these mountains are beyond all common reason, unexplainable and mysterious as life itself."

8. The power and terror of the crocodile is the centerpiece of God's revelation to Job of the wonders of His creation (*Job* 40:15–41). As in the Bhagavad Gita there is an element of destructive as well as creative power in that passage.

9. William Blake's poem is quoted by Otto's translator in an appendix on the expression of the numinous in English:

> *Tyger, tyger, burning bright*
> *In the forests of the night,*
> *What immortal hand or eye*
> *Could frame thy fearful symmetry?*

10. See *The Prelude*, by William Wordsworth, X:437–69.

11. Kant, *Critique of Judgment*, 5:269.

12. Kant made a distinction between the "mathematical" and "dynamic" sublime in terms either of huge immeasurable size or enormous power or energy. Our perception of some things as enormous or very powerful compared to ourselves arouses our responsive awareness of our own mental faculties, powers of imagination, conceptualization, and choice, and hence a peculiar kind of pleasure. Here Kant the famously rational philosopher acknowledged mental states that go beyond rationality.

13. Those on the autistic spectrum are deficient to some degree in sensitivity to other people's states of mind, apparently because of a genetic difference.

14. Hence the use of identity parades, but they are fallible because our recognition of strangers is not as reliable as with people with whom we are familiar.

15. There are matters of individual taste in music of course, but at the most basic level it involves getting rhythm, tuning, and melody *right*.

16. Otto refers at several points (39, 54–5, 165–9) to Goethe's conception of the *daemonic*, i.e., a supernatural power of inspiration (as Socrates once claimed to experience), which is to be distinguished from the *demonic* understood as evil or Satanic. Angus Nicholls concludes his fascinating study (*Goethe's Concept of the Daemonic: After the Ancients* [Camden House, 2006]) as follows:

    > Instead . . . of taking refuge behind this fear of an outside through the erection and maintenance of purely rational concepts, Goethe sought solace in the realms of the mythic, by hiding behind a rhetorical image that he called the daemonic. . . . Goethe does not regress to a pre-Enlightenment mode of mythic thinking; rather, [his] aim is to show us that enlightenment's attempted progression from mythos to logos is never complete, nor susceptible of completion.

    Goethe's more positive concept of the daemonic is akin to the exalted sense of "Imagination" (with a capital "I") in Wordsworth and Coleridge, with which I concluded "Twelve Conceptions of Imagination," *British Journal of Aesthetics* 2003.

17. Kierkegaard, *Concluding Unscientific Postscript*, excerpted in *A Kierkegaard Anthology*, edited by Robert Bretall (Princeton University Press, 1946), pp. 199–202. Kierkegaard reacted strongly against the huge-scale rationalizing and historicizing philosophy of Hegel. He is recognized as a founder of existentialism, and he deeply influenced the twentieth-century existentialist philosophers Martin Heidegger and Jean-Paul Sartre (neither of them Christian). For a clear and sympathetic introduction to Kierkegaard's thought see Patrick Gardner, *Kierkegaard* (Oxford University Press, 1988). I discuss Sartre's philosophy in Chapter 11 of Leslie Stevenson et al., *Thirteen Theories of Human Nature*, 7th ed. (Oxford University Press, 2017).

18. The "hobby-horse" of Uncle Toby in Laurence Sterne's comic eighteenth-century "novel" *Tristram Shandy*.
19. The Scottish mountains over 3,000 feet high.
20. Kant, *Critique of Practical Reason* (1788), 5:161. The whole of Kant's (mercifully short) conclusion to this second *Critique* is worth reading.

Chapter 15

1. Martin Buber, *I and Thou*, translated by Ronald Gregor Smith, with Buber's Postscript (Scribner Classics, 2000; first published in 1923). Numbers in parentheses in this chapter refer to pages of this edition.
2. As Proust documented with great subtlety in his multivolume masterpiece *In Remembrance of Things Past*.
3. Even to write of "the *Thou*" is grammatically incorrect, if we are pedantic about it.
4. Variations on the *I-Thou* theme are found in the works of others. The French philosopher Gabriel Marcel reflected on intersubjectivity and dialogue in his Gifford Lectures at the University of Aberdeen in 1949–1950, published as *The Mystery of Being: I. Reflection and Mystery, II. Faith and Reality* (Harvill Press, 1950 & 1951). These are slow-moving, subtle, and profound lectures from a bygone era, worth reading by anyone with the requisite patience and sensitivity. Marcel manages to be both existential and non-dogmatically Christian, while differing sharply from the atheist existentialism of his contemporary Sartre. At one point he wrote like Buber of "the absolute Thou (*Toi*)" (II, p. 126).

    Rowan Williams has explored the themes of intersubjectivity, dialogue, and language in *Dostoevsky: Language, Faith and Fiction* (Continuum, 2008), and *The Edge of Words: God and the Habits of Language* (Bloomsbury, 2014).

Chapter 16

1. For a compact introduction to Kant's critical philosophy see Chapter 8 in Leslie Stevenson et al., *Thirteen Theories of Human Nature*, 7th ed.

(Oxford University Press, 2017). For a comprehensive survey of his thought see the online *Stanford Encyclopedia of Philosophy* article.

2. See the general introduction to Immanuel Kant, *Religion and Rational Theology*, translated and edited by Allen W. Wood and George di Giovanni (Cambridge University Press, 1996), pp. xi–xxiv. In the event, Kant managed to outlive his royal critic and to publish on religion again.

3. *A New Elucidation of the First Principles of Metaphysical Cognition* (1755), 1:395–6; *The only Possible Argument in Support of a Demonstration of the Existence of God* (1763), 2:78–89. (What snappy titles!)

4. *The only Possible Argument*, 2:161 and 2:163.

5. *Dreams of a Spirit-Seer Elucidated by Dreams of Metaphysics* (1766), 2:372. The influence of Rousseau is apparent here. In that rather eccentric work Kant took a surprising interest in Swedenborg's claims to discern the operation of "spirits," but his conclusions were highly skeptical.

6. (1781), A592–630/B620–58.

7. Kant cannot be classed with the logical positivists, who denied all cognitive meaning to putative propositions that are neither analytic (provable by logic alone) or a posteriori (testable by perceptual experience).

8. *Critique of Pure Reason*, Bxxx. See also Bxxiv–xxxvi, B166n, and A738–57/B766–85.

9. To be developed in detail in his second and third *Critiques*.

10. *Critique of Pure Reason*, A829/B857.

11. Dare I suggest that Kierkegaard would have benefited from reading less Hegel and more Kant? He reacted so strongly against the historical and rationalizing philosophy that he encountered as a student in Berlin, but he seems rather ignorant of the Kantian philosophy that had then gone out of fashion.

12. See the rest of Kant's analysis of faith as subjective certainty about objectively uncertain matters in the Method section of the *Critique of Pure Reason* at A820–31/B848–59, and his related distinction between logical and moral conviction. I made a detailed analysis of Kant's trio of epistemological concepts—*meinen* (holding an opinion), *wissen* (knowing), and *glauben* (believing, or having faith)—in Essay 6 of my *Inspirations from Kant* (Oxford University Press, 2011).

13. *A Kierkegaard Anthology*, edited by Robert Bretall (Princeton University Press, 1946), pp. 214–15. "Passionate inwardness" sounds more exciting than Kant's cooler notion of "subjective sufficiency," but we would need to dig deeper into the thought of both philosophers to elucidate what differences there may be. At the end of the *Unconcluding Scientific Project* Kierkegaard considered the objection to the notion of "subjective truth" I raised in Chapter 14, admitting that it might apply to an enthusiastic lover, since there might be no difference between lover and Christian in respect of "inwardness." His final definition tried to distinguish the inwardness of *religious* faith from other forms of inwardness by connecting it with "the absolute paradox" and "the absurd":

> *Faith is the objective uncertainty along with the repulsion of the absurd held fast in the passion of inwardness, which precisely is inwardness potentiated to the highest degree.*

A *Kierkegaard Anthology*, edited by Robert Bretall (Princeton University Press, 1946), pp. 252–5.

14. But that leaves us with the question of what is meant by these elusive terms. Perhaps absurdity and paradox might distinguish the religious kind of inwardness from the erotic, the avocational, and the obsessional, but will it rule out religious fanaticism or religiously motivated terrorism? (Phenomena with which we are more familiar now than presumably Kierkegaard was in nineteenth-century Denmark.)

"Paradoxical absurdity" turns up again in the Russian-Jewish religious thinker Lev Shestov (1866–1938):

> *The power of the biblical revelation—what there is in it of the incomparably miraculous and, at the same time, of the absurdly paradoxical, or, to put it better, its monstrous absurdity—carries us beyond the limits of all human comprehension and of the possibilities that comprehension admits.*

Athens and Jerusalem, translated by Bernard Martin (Simon & Schuster, 1968), p. 69; quoted by John Gray in *Seven Type of Atheism* (Allen Lane, 2018), p. 153.

Critique of Practical Reason, 5:107–14; *Critique of Judgment*, 5:442–85.

15. *Critique of Practical Reason*, 5:83.

16. Though not necessarily one's own individual well-being, for Kant allowed that in extreme cases it could be one's moral duty to choose death rather than dishonor, e.g., if ordered by a tyrant to give false witness against an innocent person.

17. *Critique of Practical Reason*, 5:124–31. See also *Religion within the Bounds of Bare Reason*, 6:3–6; but at 6:139 Kant admits "an abyss of a mystery regarding what God may do."

18. *Religion within the Bounds of Bare Reason*. This work in four parts (or "pieces"), substantial enough to have been called a fourth *Critique*, was what incurred the Prussian censorship.

19. *Religion*, 6:66–77.

20. *Religion*, 6:116–18.

21. *Religion*, 6:44–53 and 6:19–202. There is also an allusion to divine grace at the end of a footnote at 5:127 in the *Critique of Practical Reason*. See my article "Kant on Grace," in *Kant's Religion within the Boundaries of Mere Reason*, ed. G. Michalson (Cambridge University Press, 2014), pp. 118–36.

22. *Religion*, 6:53.

23. *Religion*, 6:153–4 footnote. A passage in the *Critique of Judgment* (Remark to Section 86 at 5:445–7) suggests that the idea of God as a focus for feeling grateful, obedient, and humble may have a good effect in keeping up our moral striving, irrespective of the objective validity of the idea.

24. *Religion*, 6:134–6.

25. In an era when fundamentalist tendencies have re-emerged in several world religions, this hope has only very imperfectly been borne out.

26. In "Kant and Quakerism," in *Kant and the New Philosophy of Religion*, ed. C. L. Firestone and S. R. Palmquist (Indiana University Press, 2006), pp. 210–19, I suggested that Quakers (at their best) may approximate Kant's ideal of an ethical community.

27. Karl Barth, the twentieth-century theologian who reacted so strongly against nineteenth-century liberal theology, criticized Kant in his review of previous thinkers in *From Rousseau to Ritschl* (SCM Press, 1959). However Barth commended Kant's late proposal in *The Conflict of the*

Faculties (1798) for a continuing dialogue between philosophical and biblical theology. See my essay "Kant versus Christianity?" in *Kant and the Question of Theology*, ed. C. L. Firestone, N. A. Jacobs, and J. H. Joiner (Cambridge University Press, 2018), pp. 119–37.

28. That crucial little word "as" is often ambiguous between "as if" and "as, really." In this case, do we need *belief* in God or just the *idea* of God? I find a related ambiguity in the twentieth-century French religious thinker Simone Weil:

> The supernatural virtue of justice consists of behaving exactly as though there were equality when one is the stronger in an unequal relationship.
>
>   . . . He who treats as equals those who are far below him in strength really makes them a gift of the quality of human beings, of which fate had deprived them. As far as it is possible for a creature, he reproduces the original generosity of the Creator with regard to them. This is the most Christian of virtues.
>
>   . . . Such virtue is identical with real, active faith in the true God.
>
>   (Waiting on God [Fontana Books, 1959], pp. 100–1)

Would a virtuous agnostic or atheist who deals justly and shows compassion thereby demonstrate a "real, active faith in God"? In view of the title of the work from which this quotation is taken, presumably Weil would describe this as a crucial "form of the *implicit* love of God." But to have *that*, does the ethical unbeliever need even the *idea* of God?

29. John Hare, *The Moral Gap: Kantian Ethics, Human Limits and God's Assistance* (Oxford University Press, 1996) offers an extended discussion of this from a modern Christian point of view.

Chapter 17

1. Not in *I and Thou*, as far as I can see.
2. André Louf, *Tuning in to Grace: The Quest for God* (Cistercian Publications, 1992), pp. 61–2.

3. Did that tax-collector *stop* collecting taxes, one wonders? That counted as a sin in Roman-occupied first-century Palestinian Judaism, but no aspersions are hereby cast on Her Majesty's Revenue and Customs!

4. Keith Ward roams eloquently around this border in Chapter 6 of *God: A Guide for the Perplexed* (Oneworld, 2001), but returns to a personal conception of God in Chapter 7.

5. Paul Tillich, *The Shaking of the Foundations* (Penguin Books, 1962), pp. 157, 161, 163–4.

6. I touch on the latter in a non-orthodox way in "Atonement in Theology and Literature," in *Philosophy and Literature* 2015.

7. Paul Tillich, *Systematic Theology* (SCM Press, 1978), Part II, p. 205.

8. We encountered a similar theme in Chapters 3 and 4, either that everything we say about God is analogical, or (apophatically) that we can say nothing positive about him.

9. In this I can sympathize with one of Simone Weil's paradoxical spiritual-cum-intellectual remarks, which sometimes sound extremist:

> *A case of contradictories which are true. God exists: God does not exist. Where is the problem? I am quite sure that there is a God in the sense that I am quite sure that my love is not illusory. I am quite sure that there is not a God in the sense that I am quite sure nothing real can be anything like what I conceive when I pronounce this word. But that which I cannot conceive is not an illusion.* (Gravity and Grace *[Routledge, 1963], p. 106*)

Now the logician in me says that two contradictories cannot both be literally true. But if the two sides are diagnosed as having different senses, then *in that interpretation* there is no contradiction and both sides can be true (as in Kant's resolution of his third and fourth Antinomies). What then is Weil's main point here? She declares herself quite sure that her love is not illusory. But as she knows very well, our feelings are changeable and are sometimes inappropriate to their objects (one can fancy oneself in love with a person one has hardly met, and one's love for someone one does know may be tinged with other less positive feelings).

10. I venture to suggest that Weil meant that her love for God is not illusory in the sense that although her relevant mental states are mixed and changeable, *the object* of that love—the ideal of divine love and forgiveness—is not illusory, is perfect, and does not change. On the other side, she is sure that nothing real (i.e., nothing in this world of space and time, matter, and biology) can measure up to the ideal of perfect love conveyed by the word "God."This is confirmed by some other remarks of hers:

> *Nothing which exists is absolutely worthy of love.We must therefore love that which does not exist. This non-existent object of love is not a fiction, however, for our fictions cannot be any more worthy of our love than we are ourselves, and we are not worthy of it. (*Gravity and Grace, pp. 99–100)

See also my discussion of Iris Murdoch at the end of Chapter 5.

Chapter 18

1. The official title is "The Religious Society of Friends." The epithet "Quaker" arose because people were sometimes seen to tremble before standing up to give spoken "ministry" in Meetings for Worship.
2. See S. W. Angell and P. Dandelion, eds., *Early Quakers and Their Theological Thought, 1647–1723* (Cambridge University Press, 2015). George Fox emerged as the acknowledged leader of the seventeenth-century Quaker movement, but there were a number of influential voices, including women as that collection of essays shows.
3. Augustine, *The Master*, 11.38, 12.40; see John M. Rist, *Augustine: Ancient Thought Baptized* (Cambridge University Press, 1994), pp. 32, 37, 78, 89.
4. George Fox, *Journal*, 1648 (Penguin classics edition, 1998, pp. 33, 34–5).
5. Louf, *Tuning in to Grace*, p. 142.
6. Fox, *Journal*, 1664, p. 341.
7. *Quaker Faith and Practice* (The Yearly Meeting of the Religious Society of Friends in Britain, 1995), 26.63.

8. See Rist, *Augustine*, p. 33.

9. William Penn was a high-born Quaker who gave his name to Pennsylvania, which was initially a Quaker state.

10. *Quaker Faith and Practice*, 26.78.

11. To explain for those unfamiliar with Quaker practice: in "Meetings for Worship" people sit in reverent silence for an hour or so, yet it is open to anyone present to stand up and "minister" in words, when he or she feels "moved by the Spirit." Such ministry can take the form of reading a passage from *Quaker Faith and Practice*, from the Bible, or any other source of inspiration, it can also be spiritual reflection on personal experience or contemporary events. (In some Quaker traditions in Kenya and the United States, Meetings for Worship are more like conventional church services with hymns, prayers, and sermons, though there may be a period of silence.)

12. The *Advices* include a variety of uses of the G-word: "God's guidance," "all are cherished by God" (no.3), "the spirit of God" (7), "God's presence' (8), "that of God in everyone" (17), "God's gifts" (19), "God's help" (23), "the service of God" (27), "God's purposes" (35), "our responsibilities to God" (38), "the splendor of God's continuing creation" (42).

13. This is hardly the place to enter into discussion of the venerable but mysterious Christian doctrine of the Trinity. However there is an interesting approach by Nicholas Lash, a professor of theology at Cambridge, who provocatively rejects theism, if that is understood as belief in God *as a supernatural person*. Many people assume that monotheism is shared by Judaism, Christianity, and Islam (with Christianity adding in the divinity of Christ, and Islam replacing that with the divinity of the Qur'an). But instead of such a supposed bland minimal monotheism Lash proposes a linguistic reinterpretation of Trinitarian doctrine in the form of three rules for Christian discourse about God:

    (a) God (the Spirit) is to be found in all creativity and vitality in the world;

    (b) Yet nothing in the world is to be literally identified with God (the Father);

(c) God (the Word) is to be especially found in the life and teaching of Jesus.

Easter in Ordinary: Reflections on Human Experience and the Knowledge of God (SCM Press, 1988), pp. 257, 264, 276.

There is a tripartite structure here, but *not* the claim that God is three persons. In their emphasis on experience of the divine Light— or Holy Spirit, or Spirit of Christ—Quakers might even claim to be more radically Trinitarian than some nominal Christians who subscribe to an attenuated sort of theism that may amount to little more than deism.

14. *Quaker Faith and Practice*, 26.33.
15. *Quaker Faith and Practice*, 1.02:8.
16. Rowan Williams ends his little brochure on Christianity with the phrase "that energy of creative gift which sustains the entire universe," *What Is Christianity?* (SPCK, 2105), p. 37. That phrase *could* be read as referring to God as a supernatural person who creates and sustains everything. But since Williams is obviously not contributing to the physics of energy, we can take his phrase in a less physical but spiritually significant way.

    Elizabeth Maclaren voiced a similar suggestion that "God" is "the name by which men acknowledge the unthinkable, unlimited, promiscuous, prodigal resources of free life with they experience" *The Nature of Belief* (Sheldon Press, 1976), p. 25. See the dialogue in the last chapter of that book between "Snarl," an aggressive atheist, and "Swither" who expresses a vague, tentative, but hopeful faith.
17. Could this be what Eastern Orthodox tradition meant by saying that we can only know God's energies, not his essence?—I leave it to them to say.
18. Remember Kant's awe before both the starry heavens and the moral law (see Chapter 16).
19. Keith Ward's book *God: A Guide for the Perplexed* (Oneworld, 2001) covers many of the topics and figures discussed in this book, in somewhat greater detail and with a delightful sense of humor. I am grateful for his example.

An "Unconcluding" Appendix

1. For more about Quakerism, see my *Open to New Light: An Introduction to Quaker Spirituality in Historical and Philosophical Context* (Exeter, Imprint Academic, 2012).
2. *Quaker Faith and Practice* (The Yearly Meeting of the Religious Society of Friends in Britain, 1995), 27.24.

INDEX

For the benefit of digital users, indexed terms that span two pages (e.g., 52–53) may, on occasion, appear on only one of those pages.